An Exploration by the B2B Leadership Board

The B2B Agenda

The Current State of B2B Marketing and a Look Ahead

Fred Wiersema

© Copyright 2012, Gary Lilien, Ralph Oliva, and Fred Wiersema.

All rights reserved. No part of this publication may be reproduced, stored in a retrieval system, or transmitted, in any form or by any means, electronic, mechanical, photocopying, recording, or otherwise, without the written prior permission of the authors. For information regarding permission(s), contact:
ISBM
Smeal College of Business
The Pennsylvania State University
484 Business Building
University Park, PA 16802
Phone: 814-863-2782
Fax: 814-863-0413
Email: isbm@psu.edu

ISBN: 978-0-9885488-0-0

About the B2B Leadership Board

The B2B Leadership Board was established by the Institute for the Study of Business Markets (ISBM) at Penn State University in August 2011. The B2B Board's ambition is to foster fundamental advances in the knowledge and practice of B2B marketing and, in doing so, elevate its business impact.

The B2B Board engages a select group of academic thought leaders and forward-looking senior B2B executives to guide and support its initiatives.

About the B2B Agenda

The B2B Board's initial initiative is to shape a B2B Agenda that frames the prominent issues and challenges facing the B2B domain. In turn, that agenda will help establish priorities and directions for the pursuit of new knowledge and leading-edge practices.

About the Author

Customer strategist Fred Wiersema is the Chair of the B2B Leadership Board and an ISBM Distinguished Fellow. He is best known for his thought and practice leadership in the B2B field and as co-author of the global top seller, *The Discipline of Market Leaders*, and several other influential books. His doctorate is from Harvard Business School.

The B2B Leadership Board as of Summer 2012

CMOs and equivalent executive members:

Steve Erickson — Parker Hannifin
John Geniviva — Corning
Nils Gustavsson — Porex
Peter Holmes — Celanese
John Jacko, Jr. — Kennametal
Pat Kenny — PPG Industries
Mike Ludwig — WESCO Distribution
Vic Maurtua — Dow Chemical
Tom Nguyen — Westinghouse Electric
Tom Pavilon — Arizona Chemical
Jim Scott — Actuant
Sue Sears — Kimberly-Clark Professional

B2B researchers, academic members:

Mike Ahearne — University of Houston
Jim Anderson — Northwestern University
Doug Bowman — Emory University
Frank Cespedes — Harvard Business School
George Cressman — World Class Pricing
Liam Fahey — Babson College
Srinath Gopalakrishna — University of Missouri–Columbia
Raj Grewal — Penn State University
Abbie Griffin — University of Utah
Sandy Jap — Emory University
Bernie Jaworski — Claremont University
Wesley Johnston — Georgia State University
Ajay Kohli — Georgia Institute of Technology
V. Kumar — Georgia State University
Das Narayandas — Harvard Business School
Jim Narus — Wake Forest University
Ralph Oliva — Penn State University
Rob Palmatier — University of Washington
Lisa Scheer — University of Missouri–Columbia
Don Schultz — Northwestern University
Venky Shankar — Texas A&M University
Jagdish Sheth — Emory University
Robert Spekman — University of Virginia
Raji Srinivasan — University of Texas–Austin
Raj Srivastava — Singapore Management University
Tom Steenburgh — University of Virginia
Bob Thomas — Georgetown University
Bart Weitz — University of Florida

B2B Board direction:

Gary Lilien, vice-chair — Penn State University
Fred Wiersema, chair — ISBM Fellow, Penn State University

CONTENTS

PART I: Background 1

PART II: Key Findings 5

PART III: Potent Developments Are Reshaping B2B Marketing 13

    These Are Defining Times for B2B Marketers: Corporate Expectations of Marketing Are Mounting 13

    The Importance of Global Markets Creates Unprecedented Challenges 16

    Technology's Disruptive Power Could Make Certain B2B Practices Obsolete 18

    B2B Firms Are Transitioning to Align Themselves with Their Changing Marketplace Realities 22

    B2B Marketing's Role Is Becoming More Strategic 26

PART IV: The Biggest Challenges for B2B Marketing 31

    Build Stronger Interfaces Between Marketing and Sales 32

    Build Stronger Innovation–Marketing Interfaces 35

    Extract and Leverage More Granular Customer and Market Knowledge 41

PART V: B2B Marketing's Related Imperatives 47

    Demonstrate Marketing's Contribution to Business Performance 47

    Engage More Deeply with Customers and with Customers' Customers 49

    Find the Right Mix of Centralized Versus Decentralized Marketing Activities 51

    Find and Groom Marketing Talent and Competencies 54

PART VI: What's Next 57

    The B2B Leadership Board's Priorities 57

PART I: Background

**The B2B Agenda Project:
The Present and the Future of
Business-to-Business Marketing**

Through its deep connections with more than 75 corporate member firms and hundreds of B2B academics worldwide, the Institute for the Study of Business Markets (ISBM) has for 29 years offered a center of excellence most closely associated with the business-to-business domain. That domain is undergoing momentous changes. Concerned about the status quo, both practitioners and researchers have expressed the desire for more insights into what is (or could be) next. Late last fall, the B2B Leadership Board initiated a large exploratory project to address these concerns. This report summarizes the findings of our investigation.

Formally, the goal of our B2B Agenda project is to enrich views of the evolving marketplace dynamics that will face B2B firms in coming years. We regard this project as an important step in determining the major needs and most promising opportunities in the B2B domain, along with their implications for B2B marketers, academic researchers, and educators.

In structuring this B2B Agenda project, we decided to build on the informed judgments of members of our B2B Leadership Board and obtain a varied set of perspectives from accomplished senior practitioners representing a cross-section of B2B firms. We used open-ended, one-to-one interviews to gather the input, and various follow-up discussions to enrich our findings. With a deep respect for how different one industry and one company is from any other, we used these interviews to gain a clear view of the context surrounding issues and situations that arose again and again, as well as appreciate the various nuances influencing the participants' comments.

In all, 72 executives from 61 corporations participated in this B2B Agenda project, as did 30 prominent B2B researchers on the B2B Leadership Board. The executives offered the following overall profile:

- Top managers, including Chief Marketing Officers (CMOs)/senior-most marketers (41% of participating executives), other ranking marketing executives (35%), and senior line executives (8%).

- Representing a cross-section of B2B firms: industrial businesses (43% of firms), technology firms (23%), B2B service providers (21%), and diversified & other companies (13%).

- Mostly large businesses with revenues of $10B+ (26% of firms), $2.5–10B (34%), or $1–2.5B (18%).

In our judgment, the companies represented were above-average performers—including a substantial number of market-leading businesses and firms that displayed advanced practices and noteworthy experiences. Although these participants were predominantly U.S.-based and from large companies, our findings in the aggregate provide a textured snapshot of what is on the minds of an accomplished group of forward-looking practice and knowledge leaders across the B2B domain.

We expect that these findings will stimulate further action and exploration of the key challenges and imperatives that we outline, as well as more scrutiny of the issues, viewpoints, and interpretations that we report herein. An inquiry of this nature is bound to

> Our findings in the aggregate provide a textured snapshot of what is on the minds of an accomplished group of forward-looking practice and knowledge leaders across the B2B domain.

The Approach

To begin, we used a quasi-Delphic process to solicit two rounds of input from the 30 academic members of the B2B Board. They identified and defined key B2B topics that they believed were most salient. Next, we explored these topics in depth through open-ended, one-on-one interviews and additional interactions with 71 B2B executives—predominantly CMOs and other senior-most customer-facing executives, as well as other seasoned marketers in a diverse range of 60, predominantly large businesses. About half of the executives we approached readily agreed to participate (and the response among the senior-most marketers was even higher). We were pleased to find just how keen these experienced marketers were to share their views, and just how candid their comments were.

With a content analysis of the in-depth interviews, we extracted many deeper insights that helped shape our findings. We discussed these interim results during a working session with a subset of our B2B academics, and then in a roundtable meeting with 15 CMOs, which helped us calibrate the findings. A final draft of the key findings was reviewed with B2B Leadership Board members as well.

In preparing this project report, we elected to make practitioners our primary target, even with the full recognition of the valuable input of the B2B Board's academic members and the need for a further specification of the project's implications for B2B research and education.

The B2B Agenda project was orchestrated by Fred Wiersema, Chair of the B2B Leadership Board, who also conducted all interviews and authored the final document. The inquiry built greatly on the viewpoints and experiences of B2B board members, corporate interviewees, and many insightful others; however, the final analysis and interpretations are his.

provoke thought and discussion rather than provide definitive answers. That is why we call this the B2B Agenda: It brings up key issues that merit attention and that need to be addressed, rather than offering a generic set of ready-made prescriptions.

Why We Need B2B-Specific Insights

This project shines the spotlight directly on B2B-specific, rather than general marketing-related, issues. This important focus is overdue for several reasons. First, in spite of B2B's enormous footprint in the economy (e.g., making up more than half of the U.S. gross domestic product) and the challenging marketplace pressures that it helps address, the B2B marketplace and B2B marketing are simply not getting as much focused attention as they require and deserve. Many reports, conferences, surveys, and trend studies that deal with customer-related topics serve up findings and prescriptions better suited for companies that sell to consumers (i.e., B2C firms) rather than companies marketing to other businesses and organizations (i.e., B2B firms). In many cases, potentially useful B2B insights disappear from or get buried deep within marketing-focused publications, or the B2B and B2C findings become so intermingled that the results are rendered virtually meaningless to B2B firms. Academic research in marketing similarly is geared toward B2C rather than B2B issues.

Second, plenty of marketing-related insights and findings have broad applicability, but others are simply not pertinent in B2B settings. Consider the widespread assertion, from just a few years ago, that CMOs were suffering dramatically shorter tenures. The chief marketers were in trouble, and by implication, so was marketing. Never mind though that the findings on which this dire warning was based came from 100 brand leaders, operating mostly in the B2C realm. When everyone calmed down a bit, similar analyses in subsequent years showed far less gloomy results. But the episode didn't do much to bolster marketing's reputation, whether in B2C or in B2B.

> In many cases, potentially useful B2B insights disappear from or get buried deep within marketing-focused publications

In other instances, certain marketing-related developments gain a lot of attention in the business press but have altogether different implications and likely applications in a B2B context than in the B2C realm. Some notable examples include the highly touted promise of big data and social media. Impressions about marketing in general can detract from or distort what's really going on in the B2B marketing undertaken by forward-looking companies today, as portrayed in this report. We hope this effort helps set the story straight.

Third, even a cursory look at B2B companies shows the wide variation in their market conditions and business practices. "One-size-fits-all" perspectives and generalizations are bound to overlook situation-specific conditions. Framing the issues and particular settings properly is important—or to quote computer guru Alan Kay, "context is worth 80 IQ points." That would seem like an apt motto for the B2B domain. To illustrate, the various challenges and imperatives that emerged from our B2B Agenda project play out differently in traditional industrial markets compared with technology-driven settings and B2B services. In the latter category, we noted distinct differences between business service providers and those offering professional services. Customer behaviors are bound to differ across B2B buying situations, customer types, cultures, and markets, yet an up-to-date typology that considers these varying conditions remains undeveloped. In the latter part of this report, we add further texture to the various main themes we will discuss next, and we provide perspectives on the key issues from a variety of angles.

> "One-size-fits-all" perspectives and generalizations are bound to overlook situation-specific conditions.

Companies Represented in Our B2B Agenda Project

A. Schulman	Diversey	Parker Hannifin
Actuant	Dow Chemical	Philips Respironics
Agilent	DuPont	PlyGem Industries
AkzoNobel	ExxonMobil Chemical	PolyOne
Analog Devices	General Electric	Porex
ARAMARK	GlaxoSmithKline	PPG Industries
Arizona Chemical	gyro:	Presidio
Arkema	IBM	Prime Therapeutics
Bayer MaterialScience	Indium	Rogers
CA Technologies	Kennametal	SAP
Carpenter Technologies	Kimberly-Clark Professional	Sherwin-Williams
Celanese	LexisNexis	Slack and Company
CenturyLink Business	LORD	Solutions Insights
CIGNA	Makino	Tellabs
Cisco Systems	Microban	Timken
Cognizant Technologies	Motorola Solutions	UBS
Corning	Nalco	Unisys
CSI	National Starch	WESCO Distribution
Dell	New Pig	Westinghouse Electric
Deloitte	Owens Corning	Xylem
Deltek		

PART II: Key Findings

This report sheds light on the mounting pressures and demands facing B2B companies today and in years to come, many of which are quite distinct from those that affect B2C firms. Our findings adopt a senior marketing practitioner's perspective. We did not attempt to find out whether and to what extent other corporate functions hold similar views. Given how marketing is intertwined with the rest of the firm, that topic deserves serious follow-up attention.

Neither have we tried to reconcile our findings with what has been said and written elsewhere (by academics, business authors, or consulting and advisory firms) or to provide an inventory of companies' best practices in each of the identified areas. Those are worthwhile tasks for further exploration but are beyond the scope of what we set out to do in this initial exploration.

These are defining times for B2B marketers. Corporate expectations from marketing are mounting, and the stakes are getting higher.

Increasingly difficult marketplace conditions and momentous changes in customer needs are moving the spotlight toward customer-related challenges and thus onto marketing.

Striking in our interviews was how many people mentioned that their marketplaces were transforming and their business practices being reshaped. Topics related to change and transitions came up in interviews with no less than 80% of the firms we canvassed. The percentage remained similar whether we considered industrial, technology, or B2B service firms, even though the specific dynamics of these settings varied widely.

Some mega-trends are profoundly reshaping marketplaces and customer needs. Executives in 46% of the companies we spoke with brought up a host of technology-induced, macro-economic, demographic, and other trends as significant for their businesses, today and in the future. Many of these executives were acutely aware that the status quo in their industries or companies was not sustainable, which meant a need for transformational change. But they also displayed ambivalence regarding how these trends might play out—and just what could be done to address them.

Key Finding 1

With B2B markets in a state of flux, there is a growing sense of urgency and pressure on customer-related functions—and in particular, marketing—to rise to the resulting challenges.

No matter the dynamics, the prevailing (though not universal) view was that top executives had come to recognize marketing and customer issues as pivotal to their firms' performance. With that growing recognition, marketing is gaining visibility in many firms, while simultaneously coming under greater scrutiny from the top. In short, corporate expectations of marketing are mounting even as the stakes grow ever higher.

With B2B markets in a state of flux, there is a growing sense of urgency and pressure on customer-related functions—and in particular, marketing—to rise to the resulting challenges.

Considering the changing marketplace, together with growing pressures from both customers and competitors, it should come as no surprise that B2B marketing is undergoing a transformation. In the great majority of firms in our inquiry, the responsibility of the marketing department had evolved well beyond the outdated depiction of B2B marketers as folks who put together brochures and drum up leads. More pertinent portrayals revealed B2B marketing personnel as custodians of customer value, the voice of the market, or the function that monetizes customer relations. The firms in this project engaged in a wide array of marketing initiatives aimed at breaking new ground. If anything, we encountered a proactive, well-motivated group of marketing professionals that belied all the old stereotypes.

> *Marketing is given opportunities in many B2B firms today, and in these companies the jury is out—either it rises to the challenge, or it is bye-bye. Marketing has to deliver—and deliver sooner rather than later.*
>
> —Senior marketing executive, global industrial firm

Having said that, the transformation of B2B marketing remains very much a work-in-progress. Different firms are following different paths and a multitude of approaches on their journeys, with varying degrees of success and progress. To help them along, some marketers have drawn on external resources, such as the ISBM, business-to-business consultants, and educators, to leverage existing insights and prior experiences. Overall though, much insight remains to be uncovered and explored, to learn from both other firms' journeys and the often undiscovered riches available in B2B research.

Resource and time constraints created major hurdles for several marketers. They acknowledged the need for change, yet noted that their schedules had no slack, their staff was already overcommitted, or their pursuit of customer imperatives and growth was difficult to reconcile with the near-term, cost-obsessed, and efficiency-driven orientation of their firms.

Several executives mentioned that the B2B field, unlike consumer marketing, suffers from a limited cache of relevant case studies, inspiring stories, or role models. This gap could be due to the diversity of unique business conditions that B2B marketers face, which demand more situation-specific approaches and hinder transfers of insights or experiences.

Another plausible interpretation is that B2B marketing simply is moving through a growth stage, in which it has not yet reached maturity. In this view, it will take some time before commonly accepted, well-proven practices and dominant designs emerge. In the meantime, we should not be surprised to encounter a higher degree of uncertainty, experimentation, and fluidity than what marketers may be accustomed to finding.

Regardless of how this transformation plays out, we expect no easing of the pressure. These are, as we noted previously, defining times for B2B marketing.

Four potent developments are reshaping B2B marketing.

Key Finding 2

The 80% of firms that brought up the topics of change and transitions attracted our attention. Therefore, we performed a specific content analysis of the results from our (open-ended) interviews with B2B marketers in these firms. From that process, we extracted several key (and overlapping) developments that appear as major drivers of change in the years to come. Each presents a substantial domain for further exploration, and each has the potential to become a game changer.

- **The importance of global markets creates unprecedented challenges.** In 31% of firms—most of them dominant market leaders with disproportionate influence in their fields—the center of gravity is shifting toward new and emerging markets, rife with growth and action. The buying patterns and business conditions are distinct from those found in established markets. Emerging markets call for different approaches, and they trigger the development of innovative practices by both local and global companies. The incubation of these new insights and approaches could easily upset prevailing standards in established markets and bring about altogether new practices.

The center of gravity is shifting toward new and emerging markets, rife with growth and action.

- **Technology's disruptive power could make certain B2B practices obsolete.** Technology's growing and still-to-be-determined impact on customers and customer-related activities was brought up directly by 38% of companies overall, and 30% of the industrial/diversified firms in our project. We sensed high degrees of caution and unease, but also great anticipation about technology's current or potential implications for customer buying behavior, communications (including social media), marketing/sales automation and innovation, and the power of these changes to upset established business models and practices.

- **B2B firms are transitioning to align themselves with their changing marketplace realities.** Nearly half (46%) of the companies had embarked on a major change initiative, often referred to as journeys, or were preparing to do so. Their degree of progress varied, along with the extent of enterprise-wide buy-in. Some of the most common transitions were from a product to a market focus, or from being operations-oriented to becoming customer value driven, or toward a stronger service or solutions orientation, or from direct customers to end customers. Marketing occupies a central position in these company-wide journeys—often as the designated driver of the expedition.

> Clearer role definition and a broad-based recognition of marketing's evolving strategic and tactical responsibilities emerged as a core prerequisite of marketing's transformation.

- **B2B marketing's role is becoming more strategic.** In 48% of firms, executives talked about the need to delineate marketing's evolving role and its accountability within the corporation. Opinions varied about what marketing's desirable or optimal role should be. The marketers' views needed to align with the perspectives of others in their firms. But in general, clearer role definition and a broad-based recognition of marketing's evolving strategic and tactical responsibilities emerged as a core prerequisite of marketing's transformation.

Key Finding 3 To advance B2B practice, the biggest challenges to marketing are company-wide challenges.

Our discussions with executives moved rapidly from general observations to particular problem areas and opportunities. About two-thirds of the discussion content pertained in some way to two, mutually reinforcing challenges that emerged as pivotal levers for advancing the practice of B2B marketing. Both challenges have company-wide implications in terms of their potential impact on corporate performance and their need to be broadly embraced throughout the business.

- **Build stronger interfaces between marketing and other functions.** This demand was by far the most prominent theme, noted in 73% of the companies, and especially in our talks with CMOs: 85% of them saw it as their (and their firms') biggest lever for change, and nearly half (47%) of their comments pertained to it either directly or indirectly. Their direct reports and other marketers also saw this as their number one item, but spent less time on it (33% of their comments). Their attention centered on the marketing/sales interface (mentioned in relation to 48% of firms), and issues such as sales enablement and customer management emerged as essential for dealing with strategic accounts and key intermediaries. At the innovation/marketing interface (noted in 38% of our firms), the main issues ranged from R&D and technology-related concerns to managing the R&D–sales–marketing triad and defining the role of customers in innovative new product development. Other emphases included the need for marketing to strengthen links with finance (in particular, to create a shared view of marketing's contributions), with operations, and with the C-suite. Considering marketing's evolving role, these interfaces demand attention at both strategic and tactical levels.

- **Extract and leverage more granular customer and market knowledge.** This second major lever for marketing came up in half of our interviews. Although 43% of the CMOs referred to this topic, they tended to elaborate on it less (20% of their comments) than their direct reports and other marketers (31% of comments). The need for better customer and market knowledge also came up in various contexts. For example, changing customer needs and priorities raised questions. Evolving organizational buying behaviors and patterns also appeared less than satisfactorily understood, especially in new and emerging markets or where social media seemed likely to exert a still unknown but strong influence on customer decisions.

   But both customer and market knowledge came up mostly indirectly, in the context of specific business issues. Executives did not talk simply about "understanding customers better" but rather about voice-of-customer input into the new product development process, or the need for detailed customer data to lower churn. Among our academic interviewees though, customer knowledge topped their agenda. Both groups regarded it as essential for commercial excellence and customer growth—or one participant put it, "customer insight is the ultimate currency that we as marketers can use to show our worth to our companies."

> Evolving organizational buying behaviors and patterns also appeared less than satisfactorily understood, especially in new and emerging markets or where social media seemed likely to exert a still unknown but strong influence on customer decisions.

We regard these interrelated opportunities as pivotal priorities for both practitioners and researchers. They will be guiding the B2B Board's activities. In other words, these are the top opportunities that emerged from our B2B Agenda project. Both of them require fresh thinking, new knowledge, experimentation, different approaches, and a concerted effort to advance knowledge and practice in B2B.

Key Finding 4 Beyond B2B marketing's two pivotal challenges, there are four related imperatives.

The two major opportunities for B2B marketing—building interfaces with other functions, and leveraging better customer and market insights—are not standalone initiatives. To implement either of them, it becomes necessary to attend to other major imperatives that directly or indirectly affect them. In our discussions, four prominent imperatives emerged. Some of them appeared more salient in certain B2B contexts than in others, but each was potentially pivotal to B2B marketers' performance and their companies' marketplace success.

These imperatives are not new. Considerably more is known and more is being investigated (e.g., by specialized consultants, B2B academics, best-practice researchers) about each of these topics than what was evident in our interviews. A recurring problem, which we noted in relation to multiple topics, is that existing insights and knowledge appear inadequately disseminated—or at least, they are not gaining the broader awareness and acceptance that they merit among firms that could benefit from them.

> A recurring problem, which we noted in relation to multiple topics, is that existing insights and knowledge appear inadequately disseminated—or at least, they are not gaining the broader awareness and acceptance that they merit among firms that could benefit from them.

- **Demonstrate marketing's contribution to business performance.** This theme has been hanging around for some time—still difficult to substantiate and even harder to escape, due to marketing's rising visibility and evolving role. It was mentioned by 38% of firms, which expressed a general view that marketing and finance need to get more in synch, and that marketing should focus less on tracking the effectiveness of individual programs and activities and more on corporate-level metrics and the tangible value delivered to customers.

- **Engage more deeply with customers and with customers' customers.** Fewer people commented on this topic (33% of firms), but those who did held strong views on the pivotal importance of building longer-lasting and deeper connections with both direct customers and, as appropriate, end customers. Their comments made a strong case for extending marketing's scope and reach well beyond the point of sale. This imperative emerged most clearly in companies with a strong focus on solutions, services, and customer experiences, as well as in settings involving key accounts.

- **Find the right mix of centralized versus decentralized marketing activities.** One-quarter of the firms—mostly diversified firms, multi-business unit companies, and firms with extensive global footprints—cite this imperative. It is also a growing issue in firms transitioning toward more market- and customer-driven models. These companies are weighing the merits and drawbacks of each alternative, or some combination or compromise, and there are no apparent one-size-fits-all answers.

- **Find and groom marketing talent and competencies.** With the mounting and unfamiliar demands being placed on B2B marketing, it seems insufficient to call talent development a separate imperative. Good talent is needed in all realms. We could even make a case for elevating talent to a top position in the B2B Agenda. The B2B marketing talent pool has been and remains relatively limited; the opportunities we're facing are not. Although only 15% of firms addressed this imperative directly, many more broached it indirectly. We are left with the strong impression that this imperative could be pivotal for addressing the numerous other opportunities and opportunities we identified in this B2B Agenda project.

> The B2B marketing talent pool has been and remains relatively limited; the opportunities we're facing are not.

PART III: Potent Developments Are Reshaping B2B Marketing

The following parts of the report expand on the preceding key findings. Our comments reflect the various participants' perspectives on the main themes.

These Are Defining Times for B2B Marketers: Corporate Expectations of Marketing Are Mounting

A good way to reveal what's on the minds of marketing executives is to zero in on their comments about change and customers. The topic of change came up in four of five companies we interviewed, and the term "customer" was by far the most used word in our discussions, mentioned on average eight times per interview. By itself, that would hardly be noteworthy, if it were not for the magnitude of change and the growing intensity of market demands that put growing pressures on customer-related functions, and in particular marketing. The stakes are getting higher.

One corporate marketing executive in a global industrial firm expressed the prevailing sentiment as follows: "Marketers will be really challenged in coming years. We have to come to grips with momentous changes in the needs of customers who increasingly know more about what they want than their suppliers do." Others reinforced this point with stories of major customers whose due diligence and intense questioning of various potential suppliers gave them the upper hand in negotiations or pressured suppliers to expose proprietary processes and intellectual property to an uncomfortable degree.

> *We have to come to grips with momentous changes in the needs of customers who increasingly know more about what they want than their suppliers do.*

Marketing executives in almost half of the companies we interviewed noted that their marketplaces and customer needs are being reshaped by powerful forces. We loosely refer to these forces as mega-trends. Some mega-trends (e.g., demographic shifts, commoditization of markets) are easier to detect and predict than others (e.g., new technologies, macroeconomic developments). Even when major developments are transparent, their implications tend to be far from obvious.

Mega-trends bring big opportunities as well as major challenges. There was considerable ambivalence among the people we interviewed as to how various trends would play out by themselves and in combination, as well as what they could mean for B2B marketing. What was generally recognized however was that these powerful marketplace dynamics and mega-trends are making the status quo unsustainable and transformational change imperative.

Themes we heard repeatedly referred to incomplete foresight and a growing climate of unpredictability. Some companies took essentially a stay-alert-and-respond-fast stance, as one person called it. Others tried to be more proactive. To quote the general manager of a business unit in a global industrial company:

> Our industry is facing huge trends, like the growth of alternative energy and worldwide shifts in population density and wealth creation. We need to figure out potential scenarios and how these could unfold, and then make longer-term decisions as to which forks in the road to take—all with very limited visibility. Our decisions combined with those of other key industry players could well shape the future direction of our industry in our favor and fortify our leadership position.

Marketing was seen as playing a growing intelligence role.

As marketplaces continue to evolve, corporations come under more competitive pressure, not least because their customers become better informed, more discriminating, and more powerful. Buyers in many markets have broader choices than ever—and they don't hesitate to exercise them. We found this to be the case in both slow- and fast-moving markets. Several executives in this project operated in markets that are nearing the maturity stage of their life cycle, with fiercer rivalry and increasing commoditization creating big pressures for marketing.

Other companies were competing in marketplaces in which the innovations and science-based breakthroughs are spawning new demand and disrupting existing usage patterns. These dynamics create a need for fresh customer knowledge and insights into how to compete in such fluid settings.

Marketing executives in both mature and growing markets commented on the unpredictable and fluctuating economic conditions that affected their businesses. They talked about technology developments that could reshape marketing and sales practices, or else alter buying patterns and behaviors substantially. They mentioned that speed and agility are of the essence: Things are happening much faster in their markets, and the need to adjust, respond, anticipate, and experiment is greater than ever. As one technology CMO remarked: "The marketplace keeps getting tougher. R&D is racing to stay ahead of shortening product life cycles; commoditization is setting in rapidly;

> " B2B marketing is at the cusp right now. Either we get better at differentiation, segmenting, and branding our products; or we do a much better job at innovation. If we do neither, we'll lose the battle."
>
> —Senior marketing executive

customers put huge pressure on productivity (with working 24/7 the new norm); while marketing and strategy are critical but resource-starved."

All these pressures combine to create a strong sense of urgency among B2B marketers to tackle the changing conditions and their associated challenges.

Considering the dynamics and growing pressures that companies are facing, how are they coping? The answer, once more, is, "it depends." Some industry observers have noted that not all is well with marketing. Marketers feel beleaguered and may be losing their way. In recent years we have seen articles with headlines about marketing malpractice, the decline of marketing competence, and marketing's identity crisis. While we have little doubt that these observers and authors raised valid points and concerns, our interviews pointed us to a different, more sanguine assessment.

In any competitive endeavor, there is always a limited group of contestants that outperform the rest of the field by some margin. In B2B, looking at leading performers, rather than at middle-of-the-road or struggling firms, would lead to different conclusions. The executives we interviewed represent a forward-looking and above-average performing group. Their prevailing (though not universal) view was that top management is increasingly cognizant of how pivotal marketing and customer issues are to companies' performance. Instead of being marginalized, marketing appears to be gaining visibility and clout as the C-suite grows more aware of their firm's customer-related challenges. Furthermore, corporate expectations of marketing are shifting and mounting. As one chief marketer explained, "There is a growing and critical dependence in our company on getting marketing and strategy right. Top management expects us to get the right people, with the right skills, focusing on the most critical opportunities."

These are defining times for B2B marketing. Several people commented that in their firms, marketing has traditionally occupied a secondary or even a cameo role, but it is increasingly being cast into a more central or even lead role. In particular, B2B marketing appears to be undergoing a transformation in quite a few firms, and not surprisingly, such changes bring with them questions about role redefinition and clarification, broader corporate support, buy-in, and the like. As one chief marketer remarked, "Even with our C-suite awakening a few years ago to the notion that marketing is important, there is still a lot of confusion as to its role." The need for greater clarity about marketing's changing role was a recurring theme; we return to it later.

> *These are unprecedented times for marketers. It's like a category 4–5 business storm is colliding with a category 4–5 technology storm. The world of capitalism is growing from 600 million to 6 billion people, with inflation and overheated markets in parts of the world, and severely tested economies and governments elsewhere. On top of that, high tech is creating a virtual, cloud-based technology world, throwing customer behaviors in a total flux.*
>
> —Chief marketing & strategy officer, high-tech firm

We found that marketing is not always perceived as quite ready for the spotlight. As one person commented, "We have a real action orientation in our firm. Sometimes, marketing is seen as being too slow, analytical and ponderous." Perhaps this is a deserved perception; perhaps it shows ignorance of how marketing does its job or a lack of appreciation for marketing's analytics and deeper insights. Several people, including the B2B researchers in this project, asserted that superior customer knowledge and due diligence are absolute prerequisites to arrive at superior marketplace performance. Faster marketing decisions don't make for better decisions. For that perspective to take hold, corporate perceptions may need to shift.

These and other ingrained perceptions can be inimical to marketers' efforts to pursue the mandate and marching orders given to them by corporate. One B2B Board member spoke for various people when he observed how tough it is to create a forward-looking focus on growth in a culture conditioned to cut costs, drive efficiencies, and make quarterly numbers. In his assessment, the biggest real obstacles in marketing's transformation could be people just not having time and being under-resourced to tackle the big issues.

Several people mentioned how important it was to have unambiguous and consistent support from the top to move toward and instill a strong customer or market orientation in their firms and, by extension, to enable marketing to play an optimal part. One chief marketer noted approvingly that his CEO is "walking the talk" and, by doing so, sending a strong cultural message. In the words of another marketer: "There continues to be an enormous need to convey clearly, and throughout our firm, exactly what our firm's competitive distinctiveness is, and what we want to be recognized for by our customers, while at the same time making very clear what business our company is not in." In her view, that message, emanating from marketing, should cascade down the corporate hierarchy until it gains currency throughout the firm.

> "Building a powerful global footprint is our number one imperative, especially in BRIC countries that need unique products and localized support. That requires very substantial resources. The potential is huge, but so are local demands like gathering specific knowledge and customer intelligence, sizing up potential and risks, developing local talent, and orchestrating far-flung operations."
>
> —Corporate executive, global industrial firm

The Importance of Global Markets Creates Unprecedented Challenges

In three of ten B2B companies we talked with, the center of gravity is shifting toward newer and emerging markets, and away from traditional markets such as the United States and other well-established economies. These leading companies are the vanguard. To counter the slowing organic growth in existing markets, they are staking their future on expanding the business in rapidly growing areas such as the BRIC countries (Brazil, Russia, India, and China) and other emerging and growing markets in Asia, Eastern Europe, Africa, and Latin America.

Noting the vast potential of these regions, several participants remarked that U.S. manufacturing exports to emerging and newer global markets are growing at double-digit rates. Emerging and industrializing economies reportedly represent a multi-trillion dollar opportunity for B2B firms. Most of the economic activity in industrializing countries around the world is B2B rather than B2C, focused mainly on infrastructure expansion. There is a huge demand for energy, construction, and factories, along with the related machines, products, and services to run them.

The opportunities are big, and marketing's role is substantial. To quote an executive in a diversified products firm:

> China is a good example. We are riding two trends there that are important for sectors that our company is strong in, one of them being life sciences. First, the population is aging—people are living longer. Second, the middle class is expanding. These trends are spurring demand for manufactured products and related investments. We have put dedicated teams in place to research specific opportunities and gaps in these markets, carry out market segmentation and market mapping work, and then zero in on select offerings that fit well with our company's capabilities. We are trying to find new markets for existing products, but also identifying new product opportunities specifically for these areas.

Some firms adjust their existing marketing practices and methods to the newer markets; others are going a step further and developing highly tailored and sometimes new approaches, with marketing and sales placing emphases on unique products and approaches for individual markets, backed up by localized support. Rather than rely on existing capabilities and resources, companies are building commercial operations from scratch. Their focus is shifting from exporting to putting local teams in place to build products locally for local markets—which helps them bridge geographical and cultural distances. Thus, the focus is on close involvement in particular markets, rather than staying at arm's length. As one interviewee explained, "There is a limit to what you do from headquarters. The real action is in the region, and unless you're attuned to that, other companies including local firms will run circles around you."

Our interviews make clear that the challenges are multifold and sometimes unprecedented. Marketers are being asked to orchestrate activities in a diverse range of evolving regions, with often unfamiliar and changing buying patterns, distinctly different ways of doing business and new demands. They are competing

> *"My belief is that B2B is on the verge of a demand explosion for which existing organizations in established markets and certainly the ones in emerging markets are not prepared. B2B organizations need new concepts, approaches, and methodologies to deal with the speed of development in these new markets, the networked systems being employed, the entrepreneurial management systems being used, and so on. In short, organizations need to re-think the whole idea of how they go to market, the processes and systems they use, and the marketing methods which are appropriate."*
>
> **—B2B Board academic member**

with other firms, including local businesses, that are experimenting with new approaches and technologies and that are equally (if not more) motivated to exploit the opportunities. Innovation is rife in these settings, spurring the incubation of new insights and practices that could well upset the prevailing ones in established markets.

Reflecting on these dynamics, both practitioners and researchers raised concerns about B2B marketing's level of preparedness to address the opportunities effectively. Several people strongly suggested the need for new insights, concepts, and practices to keep up.

Another B2B Board member pointed out the need to learn more about the role that governments play (or could play) in establishing and growing business markets in their area, as well as to explore the interface between governments and B2B firms.

We were left with the impression that B2B marketers—both practitioners and researchers—are only beginning to appreciate the magnitude of the potential and challenges that lie ahead in global markets. We anticipate that these global developments will open expansive new frontiers in B2B practice.

Technology's Disruptive Power Could Make Certain B2B Practices Obsolete

> *Technology, pure and simple, is driving today's and tomorrow's B2B markets and marketing systems.*
>
> —B2B Board academic member

As one of the B2B Board's academic members put it concisely, marketers should not try to hold on to existing methodologies and concepts, made quickly obsolete by technology, real-time interactions, massive amounts of information available to buyers, and emerging networks and consortia. In almost two out of five companies in our project, technology was viewed as a potent force that should put B2B marketers on the alert, considering its disruptive potential to transform future business-to-business practices and interactions. People showed great anticipation but also trepidation as to how, when, and where technology developments might affect their particular industry or company over time. Nobody questioned technology's potency, but several people observed that its impact in B2C settings was easier to envision and act on than in B2B.

Our comments address three broad areas of technology impact: buying behavior, information-aided marketing processes, and emerging business models. Each of these areas lends itself to considerably more in-depth discussion, which is beyond the scope of this investigation. Instead, the observations that follow are meant to give a general sense of what is (and is not) on the minds of the B2B marketers in our companies.

Information Technology's Implications for Buying Behavior

The most commonly mentioned technology-related topic was the implications for buying behavior, resulting from the ready access that customers have to information about various suppliers' offerings and sometimes even other buyers' experiences. Thus equipped, customers can make more informed choices while increasing their buying power.

These customers also rely less and less on traditional sources—such as trade shows, catalogs, trade publications, or intermediaries—than on the Internet to stay informed. This change is altering the role of salespeople and channels in customers' decision processes and buying behaviors. It is also shifting part of the sales force's role as an information conduit to other channels more readily managed by marketing, including websites and digital media.

To quote a marketing communication executive from the manufacturing industry: "In the past several years, we have moved away from shotgun communications to very focused digital communications; we have also cut down on the number of trade shows because they have become less important for buyers. We are still in the process of rebalancing our marketing communications between traditional print and electronic media." He was by no means alone in wanting to learn more and experiment more to keep up with customers' changing buying patterns.

> Several people admitted that their increasingly sophisticated buyers grasp the value and power of technology and information much better than they do.

The impact of information access on buying decisions is better understood in the B2C field, which abounds with e-commerce and other advanced applications. The application and adoption of a similar logic in B2B is still evolving. Several people admitted that their increasingly sophisticated buyers grasp the value and power of technology and information much better than they do. More than a few talked about having rather limited knowledge of customers' buying decisions and the role and impact of information in these decisions.

Adding a further level of complexity is the rapid expansion of social media and other networking and community-creating technologies. Most activity on this front continues to take place in B2C fields, but it is starting to emerge in B2B interactions, for which the applications tend to vary from those familiar in B2C discussion. Some B2B marketers we talked with are relatively ahead in exploring the new opportunities, with considerable success. More commonly though, B2B firms are only beginning to get attuned to the new technology's potential.

Typical was the perspective of a CMO in a high-tech company:

> The engagement practices and models of customers are changing due to their growing use of social media, which influences buying behaviors in ways we do not yet understand well. In the past, we would know what channels were used by buyers and what media and influences were taken into account by different customer types and groups. Today, it is far less transparent—and far harder to monitor or influence.

Another CMO explained: "We see web-based 'power evangelists' emerging. The people can have very considerable influence, yet with social media we have no message control. So we are monitoring chat rooms and blogs, to be aware of what they say about us."

Information-Aided Marketing Processes

For decades, technology providers, consultants, and business writers have devoted significant attention to processes such as customer relationship management (CRM), sales force automation, data mining, and the like. The rise of on-demand, remotely accessed software and data (e.g., SAAS, or software as a service) is another development that looks promising for B2B marketing. Considering how much activity is taking place, we were surprised at how few times the topic came up in our interviews. Like the dog that didn't bark in the Sherlock Holmes story, the (relative) silence on this topic was puzzling. We can offer only a few thoughts on the basis of what we did hear.

Marketing technology may be a blind spot.

The first is our concern that this topic simply was not on many B2B marketers' minds. It is possible that marketing automation is more widely used than was apparent from our interviews, with the B2B people simply not bringing it up as one of their top issues. In that case, what should we make of the comments of the CMOs of two well-respected market-leading companies—the only two people who even mentioned CRM systems? One commented, "we are seeing the impact of CRM and other technologies in the sales area. Yet in marketing, how we collect and use data has barely budged. There is a lot of info, but many of our practices are still underdeveloped." Another CMO noted that the company was still struggling with its adoption of a CRM system and trying to figure out its potential to better understand and track customer needs. Maybe then the respondents did not mention marketing automation tools because these B2B companies are not exploiting those tools to their fullest advantage. Marketing technology may be a blind spot.

A second, more uplifting observation came from one of the academic B2B Board members, who noted the potential of information technology to break down interorganizational barriers, particularly those between marketing and sales. By connecting or integrating marketing and sales systems, marketing might gain greater visibility into CRM-enabled customer data, whereas sales would be able to move back into the sales funnel and open a window into strategic planning activities. Some B2B firms appear to be following this path, which suggests optimism for the promise of these and related uses of technology.

> By connecting or integrating marketing and sales systems, marketing might gain greater visibility into CRM-enabled customer data,

As a third thought, we heard from a few strong advocates of "big data"—that is, of mining large databases to extract deep customer insights. In the B2C field, the topic of big data is highly touted, and large databases are far more commonly available. But B2B applications appear more limited. We mostly found big data in settings where B2B firms needed in-depth knowledge of their customers' customers and end-users. For example, healthcare providers with corporate customers saw big data and their associated analytics as potential game changers in the years to come, allowing them to track in detail the insurance needs of the employees of their corporate customers. With these deep insights, the healthcare providers gained an angle to influence the employees' needs for and usage of their services. As another example, pharmaceutical firms worked to extract more insights from patients' (and medical service providers') experiences with their products.

Technology and Emerging Business Models

We had some mind-expanding discussions with marketers who were on the cutting edge when it came to technology's impact on business models and customer–supplier relationships. All but one of them represented high-tech companies. To B2B marketers for whom social media and big data are stretch concepts, the observations and vision of a not-too-distant future provided by these cutting-edge marketers could be downright overwhelming. Yet a simple extrapolation of current trends suggests than their projections are more than plausible.

> In a world interconnected through technology, new corporate structures and entirely different buyer–supplier configurations must result.

Particularly insightful were the comments of the CMO of a technology company who was clearly steeped in the topic. He noted that "a huge shift was underway toward virtualization—of technology, of business processes, of organizational models, and of ecosystems such as supply chains." The technology that resides in a remote place (the cloud), yet instantly accessible through the Internet and mobile technology, from anywhere at any time, is eliminating the physical constraints of geography and co-location. In a world interconnected through technology, new corporate structures and entirely different buyer–supplier configurations must result. The restructuring of customer engagement and value delivery systems could open up vast new vistas.

A lot of these trends are in their early or even nascent stage, and they may come as a total surprise to B2B marketers, in terms of the speed and the direction in which they develop. The structural shifts that may result from virtualization processes easily could affect B2B more than it does B2C. The potential power of technology to make current B2B practices obsolete is enormous. So the message is unambiguous: Don't get blindsided.

B2B Firms Are Transitioning to Align Themselves with Their Changing Marketplace Realities

Almost half of the participating B2B firms said that they had, in recent years, embarked on major market-oriented change initiatives, or were about to do so.

One particularly noteworthy finding in this project is that almost half of the participating B2B firms said that they had, in recent years, embarked on major market-oriented change initiatives, or were about to do so. Also referred to as journeys, these efforts invariably entailed a reorientation toward more customer-focused ways of running the business, with the intent to become better aligned with changing marketplace realities and opportunities. Although marketing competence building was a major component of these journeys, their scope commonly extended well beyond the marketing area. To quote the CMO of an industrial systems business, "A key part of our story is focused on amplifying the customer voice beyond marketing and the sales force." Commonly, the ambition was to transition entire business models from an internally driven focus on products or operations to an externally driven focus on customers.

Customer focus is hardly a novel concept. So what took B2B firms so long to embrace this notion? Our interviews suggest that part of the answer is that companies felt less urgency to do so. In addition, it is never easy to change deeply rooted practices, and ultimately the company's prevailing mindset and culture. Even well-intended efforts to focus on customers may have fallen short of the critical mass and determination needed to confer a sustainable competitive edge.

We suspect that the more taxing marketplace conditions and changing customer demands, as noted by many respondents, created an important impetus for companies to put a stronger emphasis on customer-oriented initiatives. Another inducement could be that companies were learning more about the journeys undertaken by their counterparts, which could have motivated them to embark on their own journey. In support of the latter view, an important catalyst, as mentioned by several practitioners whose companies were ISBM member firms, was ISBM's concerted effort to get its member companies to share what they had learned on their journeys.

In turn, several generalizations could be extracted from our interviews.

- **Corporate journeys often pivot on the marketing function.** These journeys inherently deal with customers, so marketing involvement is of central importance. In many cases, grass-roots initiatives in the marketing area or by key account management gained strong momentum and then morphed into company-wide endeavors. We also heard about several instances in which the CEO or board of directors made a strategic decision to move the firm in a different direction or build new market-focused competencies. Either way, marketing was regarded as a pivotal orchestrating function, and the need for marketers to build effective interfaces with other functions emerged as a key imperative.

- **Journeys are expeditions, not day trips.** Companies' change initiatives were mostly viewed as multi-year, concerted efforts. Senior leadership support and enterprise-wide buy-in were considered pivotal success factors. The degree of progress that these companies had made on their journeys varied widely, as did the extent of enterprise-wide buy-in. Some of this variation was due to differences in the pacing and magnitude of their planned changes. Still, even companies that had been on a journey for several years commented that a lot remained to be done for them even to stay the course, and especially to deal with economic upheavals and fluctuating business conditions.

- **B2B executives expect that their journeys will (re)shape marketplace dynamics.** When we asked people what factors would most likely help a company outperform its peers in the next five years, they commonly mentioned the successful outcome of customer-oriented journeys. They generally had high expectations of the eventual impact of their own firms' initiatives, even when facing hurdles or slowdowns. But absent success, some people ventured that a company could suffer, particularly if its competitors were able to make successful transitions.

- **Change management is a critical challenge in any journey.** A major dimension of marketers' role as orchestrators of journeys is their emphasis on change management. One senior executive in a technology business, though pleased with her firm's new practices and approaches, nonetheless mentioned the difficulty of getting broader buy-in. She and others saw this challenge decidedly as a behavioral and mindset issue, rather than a functional one. Other executives noted that inertia, traditions, and even prevailing reward systems stood in the way of change. The chief marketer of an industrial firm commented that even though his CEO advocated the transition, from a product to a market orientation, their multi-year journey had progressed only a little past its halfway point. The intractable problem was getting a mindset shift. In his words, "Our company legacy, DNA, and center of gravity traditionally resided in operations, and coming from there it is a real change to move to a market-facing model and mindset."

> The concept of customer value, so fundamental to B2B marketing, continues to elude many outside of marketing.

Moving the Journey Along

We heard numerous comments about what moves the journey along. A common thread was that journeys are not standalone endeavors; integrating them with other ongoing business activities is good for both the new endeavor and the existing practices. Here are some pointers from two CMOs. Their companies are quite different, but their comments resonate broadly:

- Continue to build robust marketing processes: train people, put the right tools in place.

- Keep working on business units' capacity to learn about and employ customer-focused insights.

- At the corporate level, find and disseminate compelling examples of best practices that have broad applications.

- Pay particular attention to your best relationship customers, because they are the ones that make your journey worthwhile.

- Collaborate closely with account management to ensure that its activities are in sync with marketing's directions.

- Get back to basics with respect to the sales pipeline; don't let longer-term aspirations trump near-term excellence.

We asked people to comment on elements of their journeys that required particular attention. Two items in particular stood out: customer value and culture change. The concept of customer value, so fundamental to B2B marketing, continues to elude many outside of marketing. Miscomprehensions can easily hinder progress, as one person explained: "Many people in our C-suite and elsewhere in the company think that customer focus means putting more effort behind sales and customer service. That fallacy reinforces our existing sales culture but does little to get us to create more compelling value for customers." According to another executive in an industrial products firm,

> far more diligence is needed to gain a better understanding of precisely what business value and impact our products can generate. Currently, customer benefits are only vaguely measured. This need is not broadly recognized outside marketing, so broader education on its importance is required. Related to that, once there is a better understanding of how and where we can deliver value to customers, it will become easier to prioritize those product/markets and commercial activities that have the greatest potential. Today, that focus is missing. Instead of prioritizing based on sound assessment of potential customer value, our company's bias is to spread its risks by broadening its portfolio.

Similar situations were noted elsewhere. The CMO of a high-tech company commented,

> we have been obsessing too long about 'feeds and speeds,' in other words product spec and technology. It seems so obvious that customers' real interest is in the results and impact that technology solutions can deliver, along with superior customer experiences. But this shift to value as defined in customer terms is a hard one for many died-in-the-wool industry veterans. Even more difficult for them is to articulate what our firm's unique customer value is along those dimensions. Their minds are stuck in a specs groove.

Perhaps the most succinct perspective came from the CMO in an industrial conglomerate: "We won't move from a sales-push to a demand-pull world until we get our technical and sales people to grasp the compelling logic of customer value."

A second key element in companies' journeys was culture change. The CMO of an industrial chemicals firm provided a good illustration:

The essential problem is that those groomed on an operations-driven model put far more emphasis on control and predictability than what is prevalent in the innovation- and customer-focused world we are moving into. It will take hard work to nudge people out of their comfort zone.

We are transitioning our organization from its past success in commodity-type offerings to a future that it is innovation and customer solutions focused. That is a huge transformation. The issues go well beyond processes and metrics: my marketing team has those pretty well covered. The toughest part of our journey is changing the culture. We are at an early stage. Our culture is still very much infused by our past operations and manufacturing orientation. Inside the firm, a short-term performance mindset prevails. Outside the firm, customers familiar with our manufacturing footprint and capabilities define us on that basis, and don't associate us with our new direction. These are strong forces preserving the status quo. A big part of the challenge is switching the corporate mindset from predictable quarterly results to the promises inherent in customer growth and longer term innovation. The parallel challenge of getting people with an ingrained internal efficiency viewpoint to start seeing things from an external and customer perspective is exceedingly difficult—old habits are hard to break. The essential problem is that those groomed on an operations-driven model put far more emphasis on control and predictability than what is prevalent in the innovation- and customer-focused world we are moving into. It will take hard work to nudge people out of their comfort zone.

B2B Marketing's Role Is Becoming More Strategic

When we started this project, a number of questions were raised. Is B2B marketing on the decline or on the ascent? Are B2B practices and knowledge keeping up with the evolving challenges of changing marketplaces? Is B2B marketing's role shrinking or expanding? What exactly is B2B marketing's optimal role? Do the answers to these questions depend on the circumstances?

In trying to answer these questions, we heard mixed messages. On the one hand, there were indications and evidence (some of it anecdotal) that raised considerable concern about the state of B2B marketing. We heard about tepid interest in B2B courses and B2B careers among business school students, marketing getting marginalized in B2B companies, companies' haphazard reliance on and poor application of customer knowledge, and overwhelmed marketers at a loss for dealing with developments such as commoditization, big data, social media, and globalizing markets. Considering those concerns, it certainly is possible to conclude, as many commentators have, that marketing is in decline or has lost its bearings.

But we can paint a rosier picture, using input from other sources, including upbeat industry analysts (such as Forrester/Heidrick & Struggles in their report, "The Evolved CMO, 2012") and companies like General Electric (with its enormous commitment to raise marketing competency to "gold standard" levels) and IBM (whose Global CMO Survey and subsequent promotional drive stress the upside potential of marketing, supported by new technology and big data).

To reconcile these differing perspectives, we purposely focused our inquiry on the perspectives of a carefully selected sample of forward-looking marketers in well-performing (and larger) B2B companies. We expected that their seasoned viewpoints would prove to be more informative than the input we might have obtained by surveying a broader cross-section of firms that included marginal performers and smaller companies.

> Our perspective provides an upbeat portrayal of B2B marketing and its future, but many challenges remain.

In our interviews with that select group of B2B marketers, we observed that B2B marketing is becoming decidedly more strategic, with an expanding role influencing business directions with customer-informed insights. Our perspective provides an upbeat portrayal of B2B marketing and its future, but many challenges remain. The preceding concerns cannot be ignored. Marketing's increasingly strategic role may be a logical outgrowth of top management's awareness of customers' importance. It is also consistent with the prevalence of customer-focused journeys and initiatives. Yet as several executives pointed out, senior teams (including CEOs) can buy into the desirability or even urgency to build a customer-aligned firm and still not understand viscerally what it entails, let alone the shift it requires in marketing's activities and scope. In the words of a CMO in a very large, product-driven corporation, "Our C-suite has nowhere near what is needed to appreciate what strategic marketing does, or what challenges we are addressing. Their brilliance lies elsewhere, as does their attention. There is often confusion as to what is marketing and what is sales, and little understanding of the different roles of strategic marketing versus inbound or tactical marketing."

> Because B2B marketing's transformation remains a work in progress, it will take time to develop clarity about its role.

We can make the case that marketing has to do more to market itself, particularly in the C-suite, but also with the rest of the organization. In almost half the firms in this project, representatives pointed out the need to clarify what B2B marketing does and delineate its changing role. Doing so would counter the considerable confusion noted around the term marketing and marketing's responsibilities, particularly among non-marketers.

Because B2B marketing's transformation remains a work in progress, it will take time to develop clarity about its role. All B2B marketers are on a learning curve—more open to experimenting, feeling their way around, and hungry to learn from other companies that are on similar trajectories. Their practices and approaches keep evolving, and determining marketing's optimal role is not a unilateral decision. Other functions' perceptions and requirements are bound to influence or even determine how B2B marketing's position will evolve. After all, in many B2B firms, the number of marketers is dwarfed by those in other functions.

One interviewee provided an interesting perspective. He imagined that marketing's transformation would play out differently in three scenarios. First, in operations-dominant and scale-driven settings (e.g., commodity products, certain business services, technology services firms), he believed that B2B marketing had less leeway to provide strategic direction and input, with pricing and efficiency-related issues probably the primary areas of focus. Second, for product- and innovation-centric settings (e.g., certain specialty firms, R&D-intensive companies, various technology businesses), he envisioned a much greater strategic role for marketing. Third, in sales-driven firms, selling through channels and intermediaries, the prevailing culture might prove resistant to having marketing take on a stronger strategic leadership role. In that setting, marketing's role expansion might be most salient if it focused on sales enablement.

It remains to be seen how marketing's transition will unfold. In the meantime, marketers will have plenty of challenges to address.

The following sampling of quotes provides additional perspectives on marketing's strategic role.

"It's worrisome when CMOs think too much like marketers, and not enough like CEOs. Unless marketing leaders focus on strategic and enterprise-wide impact, the C-suite may well shut off when the term 'marketing' is bandied about."

"Over the years, marketing has become more integral in strategic decisions on business development and technology priorities. Our next step is to get more involved in ongoing customer engagement."

"Marketing's role at a strategic level is to help technology folks and business development people focus on where things are happening or are about to happen—with a knack for spotting and investigating trends. Also, its role is important in coordinating various technologies."

"Marketing does the due diligence and rigorous analytics to ensure we stay sharply attuned to the best opportunities and the greatest value-generating actions. Those marketing roles are increasingly strategic and robust, whereas they were far more seat-of-the-pants five years ago."

"Marketing is taking on an increasingly strategic role and is held accountable for what lies ahead, with sales focusing on the current quarter. Marketing's role is to find and develop potential opportunities, and create energy around them."

"My perspective on marketing's strategic role is more encompassing that what our SBU heads see. They see our primary responsibilities as more tactical, focusing on product/portfolio management and sales enablement. I am focused on the broader issues of managing brands (corporate as well as business brands), value proposition improvement, and the voice of the customer."

"Regarding marketing's strategic role, when I see a company with marketing reporting to a VP of sales and marketing, I wonder whether marketing has a real voice, or whether it is just viewed as a sales support activity. In that case, marketing doesn't really have a seat at the table in the C-suite."

PART IV: The Biggest Challenges for B2B Marketing

It is easy to get too close to see the bigger picture. That happened in many of our earlier interviews. The discussions would readily (and sometimes too quickly) veer from broad challenges and changing demand conditions to issues-of-the-day, tactical programs, and executing well. On the latter set of topics, there was no lack of information, but fewer firm insights emerged on the former topics. Only after meeting with a group of CMOs to review preliminary findings did the myriad of dots start to become connected.

We realized that B2B marketers who appeared best prepared to deal with the new market realities were invariably well connected with the rest of the firm. References to other functions—sales, innovation, finance, operations—permeated their interviews. The marketing groups making less progress were the more insular ones, centered on the marketing function more than the business and hoping, as one CMO put it, "that by doing a lot of different customer-related things and tossing issues over the wall to the operations people and engineering, something will stick."

From this realization, two mutually reinforcing challenges emerged as pivotal levers to advance B2B marketing. First, there is the need to build stronger interfaces between marketing and other functions, particularly sales and innovation. In effect, those functions and the C-suite are marketing's internal customers. As one CMO put it, "One of our goals is to make marketing more valuable to the sales force, solving their problems and not our own." Her words apply equally to other functions. Considering that these functions are also under mounting pressure to perform, it behooves marketing to be closely attuned to their needs.

Second, it is necessary to leverage marketing's knowledge of customers—its most significant asset—throughout the organization and inject a customer-informed perspective that aligns firms better with the opportunities of changing markets. One senior marketer summed up the challenge:

> We need to develop better ways to harness and disseminate our marketing knowledge to other functions in the company. Also, we need more and better collaboration

> *"Marketing needs to get out of its silo. Instead of being marketing focused and worrying about their own function, they need to become market focused and worry about their company's performance."*
>
> **—CMO, high-tech firm**

> To advance B2B practice, marketing's biggest challenges are company-wide challenges.

inside the company and with customers and others to jointly create new insights. This sounds obvious, but not even the large consulting firms have truly figured out how to do this. There are lots of insights that remain untapped or undiscovered. It makes me think of Xerox's Palo Alto Research Center, flooding with brilliant concepts, but unable to put them to use until Apple commercialized their inventions and ideas.

To advance B2B practice, marketing's biggest challenges are company-wide challenges.

Build Stronger Interfaces Between Marketing and Sales

"Nowadays, any company you talk to wants to break down interorganizational barriers," observed one of our B2B Board academics. That is a fair comment, particularly as it relates to marketing and sales. In 48% of our companies, the marketing–sales interface was singled out as a key determinant of longer-term marketplace success.

No function is closer to marketing than sales, and no function is arguably more important to marketing's performance, however measured, than sales. One would hope that the converse applies as well, though we know of many B2B sales organizations that hold a more jaundiced view of marketing. Important as it is, the working relationship of the two functions has not always been smooth and effective. Over the years, much has been said and written about the performance benefits of effective marketing–sales interfaces—as well as about the inherent differences between the functions (e.g., goals, time horizons, incentive structures, modes of operation, scope) that need to be reconciled.

Examples of misalignment we heard about included marketing wanting to "close good business," while sales was motivated to "close now"; sales exhibited a bias toward repeat business and existing products, but marketing wanted to get newer products adopted; and sales focused on products, whereas marketing leaned to broader, value-added solutions.

In spite of such differences, the B2B marketers we interviewed had relationships with their sales counterparts that they commonly regarded as workable and improving. A representative comment came from a CMO who remarked that to her, marketing and sales are two sides of the same coin, working in tandem even though disconnects still exists: "Sales does appreciate marketing's focus on sizing up opportunities and needs, and our efforts to shore up the company's innovation practices. Also, incentive alignment has been a unifier."

Asked what future marketing–sales interfaces might look like, several executives believed that marketing and sales have little choice but to become much more aligned and integrated to deal with the rigors of competition in years to come. Their growing mutual dependence could lead to much stronger or even completely reshaped interfaces.

Why Marketing and Sales Need Each Other

As is amply illustrated in this report, B2B marketing is in transition. The increasing demands put on the marketing function, along with its growing involvement in strategic direction setting and the orchestration of major change initiatives, mandate a closer connection with sales. We heard in several interviews that companies cannot have sales organizations continue to do business as usual when marketplace conditions change: Shifting strategic directions and marketing plans necessitate alignment. As one top marketer explained,

> Marketing's role is increasingly strategic and robust, for example in assessing market growth and profit potential, or in areas like value pricing, whereas it was more 'seat of the pants' even five years ago. Sales has probably evolved less over that time frame, with still a tendency to go for the easy sale—the low hanging fruits—and focus on existing products rather than zero in on new products and innovations. That needs to change.

Neither can marketing do its work in a vacuum. It increasingly requires the input from the sales function to shape strategies, along with marketplace and customer intelligence originating from the sales force's on-the-spot interactions with buyers, decision makers, and users.

Equally, the sales function is undergoing changes that make it increasingly dependent on marketing's input and collaboration. One notable trend was customers' diminishing reliance on sales forces (and channels) as sources of information or facilitators of transactions. Particularly with routine purchases or uncomplicated buying situations, technology enables the customers to find ready information and place web-facilitated orders themselves, thereby reducing the role of salespeople (and shifting the attention to marketing and IT to put the infrastructure and support in place for customers' do-it-yourself

---

Marketing and sales have little choice but to become much more aligned and integrated to deal with the rigors of competition in years to come.

activities). Incidentally, the same transformation is happening in tech support and customer service, with more recurring tasks being off-loaded to automated routines.

We heard of several cases in which the sales function's focus shifted to more complicated buying situations. In those situations, technology and automation offer customers no good substitute for salespeople's knowledge and acumen, such as is the case in settings with large strategic accounts and dominant intermediaries, or when a B2B firm's orientation evolves from a pure product sell to solution-focused offerings. A healthcare marketing executive gave an example: "Our industry is getting dominated by a small number of very large buyers. This has had big implications. Mom-and-pop sales practices are getting overshadowed by more consultative sales approaches to engage with customers." Another example came from a CMO who explained that his (very large) customers increasingly asked for more than the core product or service and instead wanted to do business with suppliers that pushed their thinking about ways to improve performance: "What we call our 'challenger sale' approach, pushing customers' thinking with new solutions, revolves around gaining deeper insights into what drives customers' success and performance, and what gets them to their next success plateau." In both examples, marketing was seen as a critical enabler and resource for the sales function.

> Where does marketing end and sales begin? Who owns and engages with the customer?

The roles of both the marketing and the sales function continue to evolve, so we see a bit of fading in the old but still very common stereotype, in which marketing plays a secondary role, "providing hum-drum air cover for sales through leads, collateral, events and the like," as one person put it. That role is being replaced by a customer-driven, rather than a sales-dominated, model with a far more collaborative interface between the two functions, often including the customer. Along the way, questions such as, "Where does marketing end and sales begin?" or "Who owns and engages with the customer?" still are likely to be raised.

Sales Enablement

The CMO of a high-tech company, coming from a B2C background, realized quickly that "consumerizing B2B" was not the right tack. The creative and communications angles are helpful but not sufficient. Instead, he noted, "The real difference that B2B marketers can make in high-tech B2B markets comes from sales enablement, essentially taking on shared responsibility with sales to develop the most promising accounts." We heard several others, from a variety of industries, express similar sentiments. Sales enablement was the operative word.

This same high-tech CMO continued explaining that his goal was to create higher, deeper, and larger customer relations with key customers: higher in terms of engaging with more and more senior decision makers and influencers in the customer companies, deeper in terms of familiarity with the broader business context and success factors driving customers' success, and larger in terms of what the company provides customers. Another top marketer was of the opinion that "neither the sales force nor customers have flexed their thinking muscles; they are often lost or overwhelmed by what is potentially ahead of them and their industries." He saw marketing as having an essential role, for stimulating fresh views and actively exploring new angles with tangible applications for sales and the customer.

Another area where sales enablement was viewed as critical was in launching new products and product extensions. Several people mentioned that a smoothly functioning marketing–sales interface was a major success prerequisite; inadequate marketing–sales coordination seriously hampered the capacity to innovate and bring new products to market. We return to the topic of aligning marketing, sales, and innovation in the next section.

> Several people mentioned that a smoothly functioning marketing–sales interface was a major success prerequisite; inadequate marketing–sales coordination seriously hampered the capacity to innovate and bring new products to market.

Build Stronger Innovation–Marketing Interfaces

Marketing needs to be much more engaged with innovation. That was the prevailing view in our investigation. As a strategic business unit (SBU) head in a diversified company put it, innovation is too important to be left to the R&D department. Something in the same vein was said years ago about marketing being too important to be left to the marketing department, a quote attributed to David Packard of Hewlett-Packard fame. The upshot of these views is that innovation and marketing cannot and should not be on separate islands—and particularly not in markets characterized by intensifying customer demands and a merciless trend toward commoditization.

Viewing innovation as pivotal to companies' growth and ongoing success, the B2B marketers we talked with are of the opinion that marketing has a central role in not only fostering product innovation but also catalyzing business process innovation. The theme of aligning innovation and marketing came up in almost half of our interviews (representing 38% of companies). People talked about the need for marketers to direct their firms toward the best market opportunities, to insert the customer's voice into the various innovation processes, to orchestrate the idea-to-

> Innovation and marketing cannot and should not be on separate islands—and particularly not in markets characterized by intensifying customer demands and a merciless trend toward commoditization.

market cycle, and, more broadly, to be the drivers of their company's transition to more customer-oriented models.

At the same time, these marketers recognized that their perspectives on the issues were not completely shared or appreciated by their senior colleagues or broadly throughout their firms. Marketing's challenge thus was viewed as three-fold: making a strong case and paving the way for customer-oriented innovation initiatives; strengthening the product innovation process; and fostering innovation, not just with products, but also beyond the lab and research center. Clearly, these marketers viewed their role in innovation very broadly.

Making the Case for Innovation

As one marketer observed, "Innovation and major change are not natural acts for B2B companies, in particular when it involves customers." This characterization may not be that far off the mark for a sizable proportion of companies; we certainly heard many comments about the prevailing status quo holding back much needed innovation. Some participants mentioned that their R&D and engineering teams were not inclined to alter established practices by taking into account evolving customer and marketplace imperatives. We heard of general managers being leery of innovation, because of their concerns about the costs of developing and launching new products (especially those with unproven or low initial demand) or their impact on cannibalizing existing products. Other informants noted sales forces that gravitate to easier-to-sell, well-established offerings rather than newer products that require considerably greater sales effort.

The challenge for marketers as change orchestrators is particularly profound when they face the cultural resistance commonly associated with business process innovations and companies' journeys to a more customer-oriented model. To address these challenges, several people emphasized the importance of familiarizing non-marketers with the notions that are on the minds of customers. One CMO provided an example:

> A major part of our journey focused on amplifying the customer's voice, beyond the sales force. Amongst other things, we set up a heavy-weight customer advisory board that meets regularly, typically for two days, to discuss industry trends and needs, customer requirements as well as developments we are involved in. The goal is to better understand what our important customers are trying to do, and then get the R&D folks to work on it.

These observations reinforce previous comments about marketers needing to prepare their companies—not just their departments—to deal with changing marketplace realities.

Strengthening the Product Innovation Process

Marketing's involvement in new product development (NPD), R&D, design, and related processes was another recurring theme in our interviews. Evidently, there is considerable room for improvement, even in firms with a strong new product record. Although innovation and NPD are extensively covered topics, appearing in an abundance of models, methodologies, and prescriptions, the track records of companies in this domain remain far from stellar. It remains a lot easier to talk about product innovation than to do it successfully. This brings up the question of whether existing insights are not being applied properly, whether they need updating, or whether entirely new insights and knowledge are overdue. This question warrants focused attention, beyond this project. At this exploratory stage we can only provide a hint of the various issues pertaining to marketing's place in the product innovation process.

We asked several marketers how they were doing in terms of product innovation. Almost all of them stated that their companies could and should do better, and they felt that marketing's greater involvement would open up a lot of untapped potential. As one marketing executive (in a very successful company known for its R&D prowess) put it starkly: "90% of all innovations are not successful, and 7 out of 10 main reasons are marketing related." These numbers may not be universally applicable (and we have come across a range of different statistics elsewhere), but they suggest that much could be gained from further scrutiny into marketing's contribution to the success of product innovation—or the lack thereof.

Companies' experiences varied widely at the early stages of the product innovation process, prior to the new product's launch. In some firms, new product decisions were made largely by R&D and engineering, with limited regard for customer imperatives. The drawback, as one person put it, is that

> Unless marketing takes on a more optimal role in assessing where the most potential is and what customers require, the likelihood of misspecified products and misprioritized markets goes up. Engineering does not look much beyond getting the product launched, and product

> It remains a lot easier to talk about product innovation than to do it successfully.

life cycle planning and management are foreign concepts. All of that has to change.

A related way in which R&D and engineering set new product priorities is by responding to what the sales force asks for, particularly in the absence of marketing taking a coordinating, integrating role. As several marketers have pointed out, a salesperson's close contact with a customer can bring to the surface otherwise hidden opportunities, but it also can lead to subjective judgments about new products. Thus there is a need for marketing to perform due diligence to size up market potential, competitive issues and customer requirements.

Other firms decided which product areas to focus on by using financial screens and hurdles, incorporating rather crude assumptions about customer demand. To quote one example, "We tend to innovate with a cost-plus mindset, meaning there is a gross margin target associated with IP development. Our products are priced and marketed uniformly across various customer types and segments, irrespective of their importance to each customer." Absent targeted marketing and value pricing considerations, product innovation is not likely to perform optimally.

> There is a need for marketing to perform due diligence to size up market potential, competitive issues and customer requirements.

Another area needing attention was the need for more and better use of voice-of-the-customer (VOC) input to guide the NPD process, with B2B marketers noting that their engineering counterparts often had reservations about its merits or used more restrictive types of customer input (e.g., total quality management–related, house-of-quality data). Once more, what struck us was the gap between the current knowledge of this important customer-related topic and its adoption and effective application.

We came across several versions of customer involvement in the innovation process—from fairly informal iterative interactions between engineering and the customer, to products getting prototyped, (alpha or beta) tested or piloted by lead users, to co-innovation and joint development efforts. Marketers generally have held positive views of these interactions and assumed that they helped them stay more attuned to customers' needs and perceptions. We did not have many data points but suspect that the future importance of such collaborative efforts could be considerable.

In terms of strengthening the commercialization stage of product innovation, the merits of marketing's interface role were illustrated by a top marketer who reflected on joining an industrial firm where "R&D used to toss new products at the commercial units, who then scrambled to go to market. I got marketing to ferret out early adopters and lead prospect, and start commercialization much earlier. That made a big difference."

As this comment suggests, synchronizing the development and the commercialization sides of the product innovation process is a concern, and strengthening the innovation–marketing interface is of the essence. As one executive in a large and highly regarded industrial company explained, "The number of products in the R&D hopper puts pressure on implementation, given the constraints in our marketing capability."

A balanced innovation–marketing interface takes into account customer and engineering considerations. Best practice companies use disciplined approaches to set priorities for product development and growth. They assess what would fit well with marketplace conditions and with the company's strengths, how to gain better insights into developing new applications and customer requirements, and what different paths they might take to exploit opportunities.

The interaction of innovation-related functions with sales came up several times. As we noted in the prior section on the sales–marketing interface, the product innovation process requires all these functions to be aligned. Several people talked about an integrated an innovation–marketing–sales triangle. As one person explained,

> One part of our business caters to some 1,000 customers with more than 100 products and 1,000 applications. The challenge for us is to ensure that the interfacing between our 100+ commercial managers and an equal number of technical and development people is improved. The real issue is to orchestrate the triangle between marketing, R&D and sales."

Innovation Beyond the Lab and Research Center

Several marketers elaborated on the need to move beyond a product-only mindset in addressing market growth opportunities. As we mentioned in a previous section, various companies are making the transition from a product-driven to a more solution- or service-oriented business model, essentially broadening their value to customers along several non-product dimensions.

As one senior marketer explained his company's move beyond the lab:

> In the past, we kept designing stuff with engineering specs that they thought should meet end users' needs. In effect, we

> *"For our new product thrust, integration is of the essence. There is a huge need to greatly improve the interface of marketing with R&D, and added to that build a stronger marketing–sales interface. This truly synergistic triangle of marketing, R&D, and sales is the desired vision, but marketing can get sidetracked when sales take their ideas directly to R&D. My marketing goal is to manage an aligned marketing strategy and steer the company where it can go, rather than leave it to sales or R&D to figure out. Marketing's relation with R&D is okay but can at times be testy. The modus operandi is that marketing creates the language between R&D and sales. In other words, it creates the sanity in between."*
>
> —**CMO, diversified firm**

had products and technologies that were in search of markets … very much the traditional way that engineers think of the world. Now and in the future, especially the digital future, there is a different setting. We need to look at a broader set of opportunities: more complex solutions (not just products), related services and software, integrated offerings, different business models to deliver value to customers. To build market dominance, we need to examine and use inference to detect customers' broader needs, not just their products.

He and others commented on the potentially large potential that such "beyond-the-lab" innovations represent, as well as on its absolute necessity to counteract trends toward product commoditization and shortened product life cycles. Three critical success factors came up repeatedly in our discussions. First, these innovations are intended to address existing and latent customer needs, beyond the product, so it is up to marketing to determine and interpret customers' perceptions of the value that such innovations provide. A related question is how customers make buying decisions for these broader offerings.

> We need to look at a broader set of opportunities: more complex solutions (not just products), related services and software, integrated offerings, different business models to deliver value to customers.

Second, the considerable increase in complexity demands greater coordination efforts for innovations beyond the lab. One CMO illustrated the demands as follows:

Our service edge focuses on multiple aspects, e.g. tech support, analytical services, as well as advice and solutions pertaining to order-to-delivery processes, logistics and the like, all of which require greater intimacy with customers. We need to become extremely well acquainted and well versed in their business challenges and how those can be addressed by our companies' products, services and now total solutions.

Another marketer emphasized that the need for agility made his company move more toward modular product and service components that can be reconfigured as needed when customer needs evolve. Another CMO talked about the significant shifts that she was making in terms of go-to-market strategies, sales training, and communications, among others.

Third, moving innovation beyond the lab requires a changed mindset and culture. Most of the commentary about cultural impediments that appeared previously in this document applies here too. To add further specificity to the challenge,

With a technology-dominant mindset, the focus is products. The fondness for products even shows up in people's gravitating to concrete methodologies such as House of Quality, Six Sigma, and Lean Processes to address their mostly product-centric issues. They feel good about the great products they have, how they work and how cool they are, while the customer is asking, "how will this make more money for me?" There are big obstacles to make the shift from products to solutions. For one, there is limited awareness (and few relevant role models) for what difference a service point-of-view could make to our company's performance. There is interest for this focus at the leadership level, but also reluctance, especially among product people when services and solutions fight what product managers try to accomplish. The service point of view is a very abstract notion for hardened product-minded managers. The related need for deeper and different VOC input also requires a reorientation. Then there are concerns about services potentially lowering gross margins, but little thought is given to the duration of the service revenue stream (versus one-time product purchases) or to the competitive edge that a total solution offering provides vis-à-vis a product-only deal. With a product-only mindset, companies become less relevant when their customers want a broad value set.

—Senior marketing director, industrial firm

Our overall impression is that these and other beyond-the-lab innovations constitute rich territory for marketing to explore and engage. Along with marketing's greater involvement in the product innovation process, the opportunities—and challenges—certainly seem plentiful.

Extract and Leverage More Granular Customer and Market Knowledge

The challenge of customer knowledge was nicely framed by a business unit head who asked rhetorically what defines marketing, then explained:

The answer is clear-cut for other areas of the business. What defines sales is bringing in revenues; R&D comes up with new products; manufacturing makes them; logistics moves them; HR makes sure we have the right people, and finance looks after the numbers. These are all pretty tangible—and you can track their output. It is not that simple with marketing. What defines marketing is customer knowledge and customer value—but customer value only happens because of what everybody else in the business is doing.

> What defines marketing is customer knowledge and customer value—but customer value only happens because of what everybody else in the business is doing.

The topic of customer or market knowledge, broadly defined, was mentioned in 52% of our interviews with B2B practitioners; it was also the top issue that emerged from our interactions with the academics on the B2B Board. One person described customer knowledge and customer insights as the currency that marketers use to show their worth to others in their company. Another person considered customer knowledge as marketing's very reason for being. In most other instances, B2B practitioners did not refer to customer knowledge as a stand-alone topic but rather brought up its importance in the context of particular marketing issues (e.g., reducing churn) or business issues involving other functions, such as sales and R&D.

We found several reasons leveraging more granular customer knowledge is a particularly important challenge for B2B marketing. First, the demand for it has increased. Marketers operate in increasingly complex, varied customer and market situations requiring more fine-tuned insights. Mutating and emerging customer needs and priorities, often in new and unfamiliar markets, appear less than adequately understood. Likewise, new developments such as social media and their implications for B2B buyer behavior raise questions but remain hard to pin down.

Customer knowledge and the related analytics continue to be underleveraged.

Second, the supply of information (often of mixed quality or from untested providers) continues to expand in our Internet- and mobility-dominated era, not just for customers but equally for suppliers. Far more information is at hand than a dozen years ago. Companies tap into nonstandard sources, such as internal transaction data or intelligence on service interactions, in an effort to open yet another window into customers' behavior. Already time-pressured and talent-starved, marketing departments are seriously tested to keep up with the flood of data and extract solid customer insights from it.

Third, in several interviews, we heard that customer knowledge and the related analytics continue to be underleveraged. The challenge, as one person summarized it, was to "change perceptions (or the reality?) that marketing's data are too soft, too generic and too late." Even when pertinent customer insights were available or could be obtained, managers acted or made decisions without using those insights to their full extent. The adverse potential outcomes of partly informed decisions were not always visible, in terms of missed opportunities or suboptimal results, which meant that such patterns could easily become pernicious.

> Customer knowledge resonates more strongly when experienced first-hand, as this CMO's account illustrates:
>
> > Just before the 2008 economic downturn, our company launched a big value-based "commercial excellence" initiative. As part of this, we instituted a strategic account management program whereby senior executives take an active role on an account team, getting involved in internal meetings, as well as visiting with the key account a few times a year. To hear the customer voice, beyond the sales force, we set up an industry heavyweight advisory board that meets regularly, typically for a few days, to discuss industry needs and trends, customer needs, as well as developments that our company is involved in. The goal is to understand much better what big customers are trying to do, and then to get our R&D folks to work on it. We are focusing sharply on what makes us more attractive than the customer's next best alternative, with concrete evidence of the impact of our products and solutions on the customer's business.

Particularly considering these challenges, marketing practitioners (and B2B academics) asserted that a focus on granular customer and market knowledge was not optional but rather mandatory in the new world of B2B competition.

In our interviews, three broad application areas were noted for which customer knowledge was indispensable, with several people commenting on more than one of them. The first area, customer knowledge in the new product and innovation domain, was addressed in our prior section on the marketing–innovation interface. A sampling of perspectives on the other two areas follows.

Changing Buying Behaviors

Buying behaviors change over time: they aren't the same at the early stages of product life cycles as at a later time when offerings of various rivals are becoming more and more alike and everyone's value proposition begins to resemble those of others. Customers' decision-making processes are also reshaped by a host of factors, not in the least by the ongoing trend of B2B buyers becoming better informed and more discerning, as well as having a greater choice of viable alternatives.

The question, "How can we get to know more about the influences and factors that customers and buying organizations consider?" is increasingly pertinent but also harder to answer with

> The question, "How can we get to know more about the influences and factors that customers and buying organizations consider?" is increasingly pertinent but also harder to answer with the numerous dynamics affecting B2B marketplaces.

the numerous dynamics affecting B2B marketplaces. Neither practitioners nor researchers appeared to have the answers. The common view was that buying processes vary a lot from one setting to another; for example, prevailing patterns in mature markets are quite unlike those in emerging markets; decision making in new high-tech markets tends to be different from those in established industries, and even within such settings, there are considerable variations. In our inquiry, it was generally recognized that an up-to-date typology and understanding of such different situations would be very valuable. The way factors such as social media's impact on buying behavior would fit into the picture was another unanswered question.

Our interviews provided the flavor of different buying situations. We heard of several cases in which buying organizations had become highly sophisticated over the years, but suppliers' selling and marketing organizations did not keep up with these evolving buying considerations and processes. Other firms whose focus was shifting from a product- to a solution-dominant model found that they knew little about how their customers would evaluate alternative suppliers. Of course, some of the customers didn't quite know what to make of their suppliers' shift to solutions either, making it even harder to understand buying behaviors.

> Customer value is B2B marketing's defining preoccupation; marketers' pressing issue is to ensure that customers derive value from the use of the suppliers' offering.

One CMO placed the emphasis on customer segmentation, not market segmentation, with the intent of distinguishing customers that valued trusted suppliers from those that simply wanted a vendor and nothing more. He considered the distinction meaningful in terms of buying processes as well as priorities, and he also recognized the great need to obtain deeper insights.

Yet another illustration of different buying situations came from a company whose 10,000+, relatively small customers were served mostly through channels and intermediaries that had little buying power. The buying behaviors of these end customers and the middlemen had totally different parameters than those of the company's key accounts.

Value-in-Use, and User Experiences

Another category of customer knowledge that continues to gain interest deals with what happens after the sale. Customer value is B2B marketing's defining preoccupation; marketers' pressing issue is to ensure that customers derive value from the use of the suppliers' offering. The challenge of quantifying that value was an operative theme. In the words of a senior marketer in an industrial firm, "We want to ensure that we fully understand and focus on what really has an impact on customers. I think we could do that better—with greater granularity, faster, and more effectively. The question is 'how?'"

One executive saw becoming more intimate with selected markets and customers as her firm's biggest challenge. She regarded greater knowledge and insight about buyers' and users' evolving needs as prerequisites to develop a stronger service edge for her company—such as by providing more tech support, analytical services or advice, and solutions to complement their core products.

In two more areas, the quest for customer knowledge was taking on new dimensions, so they became the focus of some B2B marketers, determined to create value by enhancing customers' experiences and using deeper insights into the customers of their customers as a potential differentiator. We return to these topics later.

PART V: B2B Marketing's Four Related Imperatives

Marketing's big challenges cannot be seen in the abstract. A number of related imperatives need addressing:

Demonstrate Marketing's Contribution to Business Performance

The topic of demonstrating marketing's performance contribution (or more narrowly, its return on investment) is a longstanding, even tired, issue for B2B firms. It keeps coming up as an important concern, and it is getting harder to ignore with the rising visibility and greater demands being placed on the marketing function by corporate leaders. It was mentioned in 38% of the companies in our inquiry, though with relatively little elaboration: Only 7% of our interview content pertained to the topic. That might indicate a sense of resignation or déjà vu, or alternatively, a shortage of concrete insights worth sharing.

Nonetheless, we ended up with multiple perspectives that may be of assistance in framing the issues. The first built on the comment of a B2B Board member, who said that marketers who are not getting enough recognition from the C-suite made him think of companies not getting enough acclaim from important customers. In both instances, questions could be raised as to whether expectations were aligned, and whether value was communicated and delivered properly. In line with that thinking, several people reiterated the importance of obtaining greater clarity about marketing's (evolving) role, as well as the need to have marketing focus on corporate-level metrics, not on departmental performance. As one person put it, "Marketing's goal should not be to make marketing look good, but to make the business run better."

A second refrain in our interviews was the difficulty of disentangling the contributions that marketing made to revenue growth, profit performance, or other corporate performance metrics, from that which was added by sales, R&D, or operations. Marketing's increasingly strategic role and its longer-term horizon added further complications to efforts to size up its impact.

With discrete marketing activities and program being easier to track and measure than broader-based and longer-term initiatives, companies inevitably leaned toward the former. Yet

> **"** There is a good chance when marketing's role is less than clear in the eyes of a company's leaders, that funding of marketing programs and personnel decisions is not carried out optimally, even when marketing has a seat at the leadership table and has credibility overall. We need clear-cut agreement in the senior ranks on who does what, and what is expected of marketing. **"**

demonstrating the effectiveness or efficiency of a particular effort might do little to demonstrate marketing's overall impact on the business. As one person noted, "We talk about measurable ROI for marketing programs, yet the reality is that marketing budgets in our company are discretionary and unallocated." Similarly, other marketing tracking approaches were being questioned:

> Customer profitability reports, net promoter scores and satisfaction numbers do not easily translate into corporate performance metrics that are intuitively appealing to the C-suite. Other approaches will continue to emerge as long as this is the case.

On a more positive note, we heard of highly successful customer loyalty tracking programs and of companies successfully using a battery of metrics to keep a close eye on the impact of their marketing actions. Several executives refused to see the issue as intractable. They anticipated that consultants and researchers would shed further light on the topic. If they are right, we expect to see some much needed progress on this front.

> *We potentially derive more impact from standardizing certain marketing practices across SBUs and from rationalizing our brands than from a fixation on measuring individual programs.*

The third theme related to marketing's impact focused on its interactions with finance. Both practitioners and academics pointed out that these two functions are often on different wavelengths, with potentially counterproductive outcomes. They argued that marketing could gain credibility if it spoke the language of finance better and had a greater appreciation of finance's priorities. In the same way that marketing is facing more demanding customers, finance is facing tightening conditions. "Lean and mean" is today's operative message—and not just for marketing. Tighter budgets and discretionary spending cuts provide less leeway for marketers to tackle everything they deem important.

On the one hand, by holding marketers' feet to the fire, finance is forcing them to rationalize, prioritize, and execute with more discipline than ever. As one person ventured: "We potentially derive more impact from standardizing certain marketing practices across SBUs and from rationalizing our brands than from a fixation on measuring individual programs."

On the other hand, inopportune cuts in marketing might lead into cuts in growth or worse. Marketing has a vital stake in helping finance make the proper decisions. Yet in the opinion of one of our B2B Board members, "for marketing to be heard, it needs to build stronger business cases for its investment and spending proposals."

Engage More Deeply with Customers and with Customers' Customers

The term "customer engagement," just like the word "marketing," means different things to different people. The issue of deeper customer engagement came up regularly in our interviews. Semantics aside, it was regarded as a topic of growing importance, focused on interactions with customers. One of our B2B Board members noted that "B2B marketing has always been social. Now it is getting more so." Some informants referred to it in the context of sales management; others associated it more with customer communications and social media. Rather than trying to reconcile the various interpretations, we simply view customer engagement as the ongoing, rather than one-time, interactions with selected customers, designed to nourish business relations.

The quest to build sustained, deeper connections with customers is not new, but the heightened attention it is receiving in the forward-looking companies we talked with is certainly warranted. Business publications and academic journals have long extolled the virtues of moving from a transactional or arm's-length mode of operating to relationship-based engagements. One benefit of deeper engagement that resonated strongly in our interviews was its role as a catalyst in gaining a better understanding of customers' existing or latent needs and their buying decisions. Furthermore, empowered customers continue to develop a stronger voice in how they want to interact with their suppliers, with rising expectations about the value that should be created, beyond the product purchase.

Deeper engagement was addressed in a variety of ways. First, companies talked about putting an inordinate focus on selected customers whose increased business potential seemingly would outweigh the costs of more intensive interactions. As one interviewee expressed it, "Our leadership team realized that indiscriminate 'spray-and-pray' selling isn't a smart way to build profitable customer relations." Several comments indicated that interactions with these customers were focusing more acutely on understanding and addressing pivotal requirements. In addition, they were enriched by involving other functions in the customer–supplier dialog. Some people said they were exploring how social media could potentially strengthen—or otherwise alter—their commercial interactions.

In a few instances, people mentioned that they were looking into more extensive collaborative projects and new business models that would have the potential to reshape customer–supplier relations dramatically, in areas as diverse as product development, logistics coordination, and technical service. The

> *I foresee successful firms engaging more and more closely with customers—beyond the sales force's contacts with a few people, to include collaboration at multiple levels between supplier and customer—and also via digital links, networks, and communities.*
>
> —Senior executive, industrial firm

prospect of such joint efforts represented quite a departure from traditional discussions of B2B marketing, giving us a glimpse of the future, with a lot of new potential insights.

Second, beyond this intensifying focus on selected interactions, we encountered a strong interest among some B2B firms in the potential role of customer experiences as a differentiator. Several people pointed out that customer value delivery does not stop at the time of sale but continues long afterward.

Some people, especially in business services firms and companies with a strong solutions orientation, talked about experience design as the most promising emerging space for competitive differentiation. The B2C field seemed well ahead of B2B, and thus worthy as a source of learning. They noted however that creating distinctive experiences in the B2B domain was more complex, due to the multitude of buyers, influencers, users, and decision makers that might need to be considered, as well as the challenges of getting to know well enough what each of these parties valued or disliked at various points.

Orchestrating the entire experience cycle inevitably would need overall coordination and direction. Again, we found that marketing's interactions and interfaces with other functions were viewed as a critical factor in planning, tracking, and enhancing customers' experiences.

A few people commented that more B2B firms were moving their customer service function from the sales organization to the marketing organization. Instead of being a back office function in sales, it would be integrated into marketing's efforts to manage customer experiences. As one person noted, "The quote 'customer service is the new marketing' is gaining credence."

Third, several companies took the idea of customer experience management a step further and applied it not to their direct customers but to their customers' customers'—and in some instances, all the way to end-users or consumers (an approach sometimes referred to as B2B2C). For example, we heard cases of business insurance firms that built a competitive edge with their corporate customers by providing better experiences for their customers' employees. Likewise, a business services firm catering to educational institutions put strong emphasis on enhancing students' experiences, even setting up an innovation lab to explore these end-users' requirements.

Clearly, knowledge of customers' customers could be an important asset to help B2B firms set themselves apart from rivals

> *With customer relations extending over longer periods, we want to be attuned to all critical touchpoints along the engagement cycle. Sustaining the customer connection over time is as important as doing one thing right at any given time. We are looking at ways to create value and ensure that customers derive benefits from our offerings well beyond the point of sale.*
>
> **—Executive, high-tech company**

who continue to focus solely on direct customers and middlemen, sometimes with limited visibility into where their products end up or how they are used.

Fourth and finally, we came across yet another variation on the same theme, in essence an extension of the ingredient branding approach that originated at DuPont. The suppliers experimenting with this approach demonstrated to their direct customers that the customers' product would perform better with end users if it was built with the suppliers' components, ingredients, or technology rather than with those of other suppliers. To back up their claims, they engaged closely with end customers to determine their likes, dislikes, and experiences. Once again, knowing more about the value that is delivered and perceived opens up opportunity.

Find the Right Mix of Centralized Versus Decentralized Marketing Activities

Take a look at the organizational chart of a large company with a limited number of products and operations in markets with pretty similar conditions. It should not be difficult to locate marketing. The marketing function might be separate from or combined with sales; perhaps one reports to the other. Either way, the arrangement is usually transparent. Now take a look at companies with multiple SBUs, operating in widely differing markets around the world, moving from a product-centric to a customer-centric focus, and with marketing becoming increasingly strategic. Apart from how the marketing–sales interface is configured, questions arise about marketing's centralized versus decentralized responsibilities. Chances are that it is less clear-cut exactly where marketing fits in on the org chart.

That is exactly what we found in our inquiry. Marketers increasingly occupied central leadership positions, with chief marketing officers and their equivalents getting a stronger voice in the boardroom. At the same time, B2B marketers away from headquarters are coping with mounting marketplace pressures within their individual business units and geographies. In light of these developments, what is the proper way to organize the marketing function? Should it be more centralized or decentralized? Is it advisable to devise a combination or use some form of matrix organization? Does the organizational structure require adjustment as marketing's role evolves further? Companies are weighing the merits and drawbacks of various alternatives, with no apparent one-size-fits-all answer.

> In light of these developments, what is the proper way to organize the marketing function?

We had the distinct impression that marketing's central role was gaining prominence, particularly in the most forward-looking of the companies we interviewed. Chief marketing officers' perspectives inform the processes of corporate priority setting and resource allocation with a customer perspective, while providing needed direction and coordination of corporate-wide initiatives or customer-focused journeys. Greater centralization can pave the way for the broader adoption of more effective marketing practices, lead to scale and learning advantages, and amplify marketing's strategic impact.

The CMO of a manufacturing firm elaborated:

> In our central marketing role, we are always on the lookout for potentially destructive shifts that may be on the horizon, and for potential beyond our primary offerings. In that context, we stimulate the firm to move outside of our core, taking modest risks by exploring and trying out related or even new areas. Without the CMO or similar voice, and without an infusion of customer and market insights, engineers tend to think black and white, looking for perfection, and as a result being hesitant to take on anything other than what they feel most on top of.

Centralization of marketing has its limitations. We heard of several cases in which local market conditions necessitated a level of agility or entrepreneurialism that would be hard to attain with a centralized approach. Uniform practices might not be easily imposed when local practices are ingrained. Another common difficulty is that SBU heads may resist having their autonomy usurped by a central authority. Yet a different drawback was related to us:

> We downsized the central HQ marketing function when it turned out to get dragged down into day-to-day local issues in faraway countries. We restructured that setup and set up regional marketing teams, downsizing the central marketing function drastically, and freeing up HQ to focus on strategic issues.
>
> —Global marketer, industrial firm

A decentralized approach was more typical in companies with disparate SBUs or widely varying geographies with individual P&L statements. In these settings, we found that being close to particular product markets and geographies had potential payoffs from greater speed, flexibility and local knowledge. Those payoffs trumped the advantages of scale and scope in a more centralized approach.

> **"** Our enterprise model puts corporate power behind the CMO role, as does GE's. That helps us to inject fresh thinking in the C-suite, and size up the bigger shifts and potential that are harder for individual SBUs to discern and exploit. **"**
>
> —CMO, manufacturing company with a centralized organization

> The following account touches on the centralization versus decentralization issue, and on the related consideration of marketing's more strategic role:
>
> I was hired years ago into the newly created CMO slot in our company. At the outset, there was no consensus among the C-suite as to whether the CMO should report to the CEO or not. It was decided that it should, which was the right decision, but even with that, the new position had no automatic credibility—the incumbent had to prove his merits. It took a while to figure out marketing's space. For instance, pricing decisions were made within SBUs and I decided not to claim that role, but to show my worth indirectly. I was able to build credibility by starting at the company's largest market and generating fresh insights, especially related to lead indicators pertaining to market conditions and the like. These insights proved very useful for the SBUs to make more informed and focused pricing decisions. Another credibility builder was my taking on the strategic task and due diligence of exploring which new markets we should play in. Yet another valuable role was in new products. We get marketing involved and begin the commercialization process well before the lab completes it work. Also, including more VOC input was an important move.

In P&L–driven firms with greater autonomy for each business unit, central marketing had less of a say in what each unit did. The role of the CMO in these firms was more focused on commonalities across SBUs and corporate-wide strategic opportunities and priorities. As one person put it, "our overarching central marketing function is to look for the white space between and around each business unit." With respect to the day-to-day running of business units, SBUs and regions were leaning on their local marketing groups to address customers' very specific needs for a tailored approach. In one company, individual customers' requirements absorbed some 60% of global R&D spending, creating a commensurate need for marketing to be attuned to variations in their markets.

A few companies, in both centralized and decentralized settings, established separate high-level positions or groups to complement their well-entrenched marketing groups. Less encumbered by existing structures, these setups were intended to open new vistas to scout for new opportunities. One person described her role as "customer innovation officer" by noting that co-innovation with customers was a priority for her group. Another explained, "In my newly created position as chief growth officer reporting to the CEO, I am responsible for customer growth and retention, and for business development. My corporate role is to find bright spots and overlooked potential.

> *"With some 150 P&Ls worldwide in distinctly different settings, we have a rather different challenge than what a large conglomerate with a small number of highly centralized divisions is facing—the latter can put a CMO in charge of each major group. Instead, we face the task of getting our central intelligence, marketing analytics and processes translated into local action."*
>
> —Senior executive, large diversified company

By collaborating closely with each of the divisions, we draw on a far greater range of insights across the corporation."

Whether these approaches will pan out is yet to be seen. Some companies that had tried to set up separate groups to scout for new business opportunities across the globe reported mixed outcomes, with the biggest impediment being their lack of connection to the main business. These and other experiences suggest that the topic is bound to remain on B2B marketers' agenda for some time. The search for further insights continues.

Find and Groom Marketing Talent and Competencies

While developing marketing talent is unquestionably of central importance to B2B firms, several people observed that the topic has not received as much attention as talent and competency development in other customer-facing functions, such as sales or technical service and support. They noted that their companies in more recent years had begun putting a stronger emphasis on development efforts with a focus on marketing. In general, these efforts addressed several important needs.

First, B2B firms have commonly moved people from other functions into marketing, often with little prior training or exposure to the nuts and bolts of marketing's tasks. The supply of business school graduates with considerable B2B education has been limited, and these graduates would need to complement their formal education with company- and industry-specific exposure. On-the-job grooming continues to be a mainstay in B2B, but with noted limitations. As one executive explained,

Marketers' roles are getting more and more demanding. Yet there is a real shortage of B2B marketing talent, and most companies can do only so much to groom people on the job.

With on-the-job training there is a delay in making people fully productive. Also, it can lead to inconsistent practices. We often noted uneven performance levels. That changed after we did a formal assessment of our existing and desirable marketing competence levels. We established universal performance standards, streamlined our hiring process and implemented a solid curriculum to groom our people. We put together a common toolbox and playbook to get everyone on the same page, and now are putting all our effort into implementation. Having the right approach is one thing—getting everyone to act on it is quite a different challenge.

Although building talented marketing teams was regarded as important, some executives expressed the related concern of holding on to that talent, especially in emerging markets where young professionals reportedly have greater mobility and little loyalty to specific firms.

Second, as these competency development efforts create a much needed foundation, B2B marketing's role continues to evolve. Mounting and often unfamiliar demands are being put on B2B marketing, and companies often are unable to find or groom the needed marketing talent internally.

The option of hiring people from other companies is limited by the finite talent pool of B2B marketers. Further aggravating the situation, the increased demand for talent from just a few major corporations can severely hamper other companies' hiring efforts. An example noted in our interviews was GE's expansion of its marketing staff by thousands of people some years ago, leaving others even fewer options. In the words of one CMO in a business services firm, "Real talent is sparse; hiring from B2C firms given their depth in marketing has proven to be the wrong thing to do—often B2C marketers find themselves facing a disconnect when trying to address the B2B challenges." The CMO of a high-tech company wondered whether other sources of customer-savvy talent could be found or developed:

> The talent pool in B2B is limited. It's hard to find qualified candidates in other companies. We transfer people from technology or sales, but they often lack pure marketing backgrounds or commercial experience.

> The front line, sales and marketing all need to be deeply groomed in understanding how customers can and will be affected by the megatrends we are seeing, and at the same time need to have a strong comfort level and skills with the changing technologies and business process gyrations that are occurring. Finding people with the right mindset, background, training and affinity is critically important—with MBA programs feeding some of the demand, consulting firms being a potential source, and some more specialized and focused grooming places such as the educational system in India (with its IIT and IIM) offering another angle.

Third, with marketing's role becoming more strategic, and customer-related challenges affecting not just marketing and sales but many others in the organization as well, there is a recognition that a broader familiarity with and understanding of customer-based perspectives needs to be cultivated. One SBU head we interviewed remarked that "Companies are putting their management through finance-for-non-financial-executives programs. Shouldn't they be doing the same by running marketing-for-non-marketers programs?" A broader appreciation of marketing's activities would facilitate learning from others' successes and new approaches. One person noted that in his company, the required skill set to adopt other companies' best practices was simply not there, rendering them essentially irrelevant.

> A broader familiarity with and understanding of customer-based perspectives needs to be cultivated.

Fourth, some people argued that an altogether different breed of senior marketing leadership and CMO would be needed to deal with the unprecedented challenges and opportunities, such as those in emerging markets, and in markets experiencing major technology-driven change. Along with changes in marketing's role, they envisioned the evolution of the CMO's position and profile. The roles and responsibilities we outlined in this report point to marketing leaders being orchestrators, change managers, strategists, and general managers of a kind. They wondered what the CMO of the future might look like, and what other senior leadership roles and even organizational adjustments might be on the horizon.

These observations raise a lot of topics for further thought. Together with the other input we obtained during our investigation, they take us a step forward in our understanding of what is happening in B2B marketing today, and what lies ahead.

PART VI: What's Next

This exploratory project has helped us get a clearer picture of the major forces and developments affecting business markets, as well as their implications for marketing. To sum up, we found that B2B markets are undergoing major changes and that evolving customer demands are placing unprecedented pressures on B2B marketing and other customer-facing functions. Two big challenges emerged from our inquiry (strengthening marketing's interfaces and leveraging granular knowledge), along with four related imperatives for B2B marketing (i.e., demonstrating its impact, deepening customer engagement, organizing marketing, and developing talent/competency). Together they represent a important set of issues for practitioners and researchers to put on their B2B agenda.

Among the rich diversity of business conditions, practices, and situation-specific nuances we encountered, two major challenges stood out and were widely regarded as pivotal levers for advancing the practice of B2B marketing. Both these challenges are company-wide and interconnected rather than isolated tasks. The more effectively these challenges (and related imperatives) are addressed, the greater their potential impact on business performance.

- **Build stronger interfaces between marketing and other functions.** This drive is particularly important, considering B2B marketing's evolving and increasingly strategic role in demanding marketplaces. Marketing derives its impact from its ability to interact with and add value to the activities of other areas of the firm, most notably the marketing–sales interface, the innovation–marketing interface, and its connections with finance and the C-suite.

- **Extract and leverage more granular customer and market knowledge.** Customer-related information can be seen as marketing's primary asset, yet it is variously underutilized, ill-suited, or insufficient to help companies get better aligned with their evolving marketplace opportunities.

These two challenge areas are very broad, and the nature of our B2B agenda project did not lend itself to further delineation of specific issues for practitioners to explore, or for academics to

The B2B Leadership Board's Priorities

research. That is our next step. We will focus the B2B Leadership Board's ongoing efforts, as well as the ISBM's academic funding activities, on two priority topics within these broader challenges:

1. **The innovation–marketing interface and its connection with sales** (referred to as the innovation–marketing–sales triangle in our interviews). We see innovation as a particularly salient topic for marketing. Considering the profound changes that are occurring in B2B marketplaces, the innovation–marketing interface will be integral in shaping the next chapter of B2B practice.

2. **Organizational buying behavior.** While buying patterns are evolving greatly, our knowledge and models have not kept up with the dynamics of changing and emerging markets, influential factors such as new technologies and social media, and cross-industry differences. We are in need of new insights and an up-to-date taxonomy as a foundation for future research and practice enhancement.

The Innovation–Marketing Interface: Our Next Steps

The B2B Leadership Board will pursue a dual set of activities to assess emerging practice needs and capture current research insights. By identifying and highlighting specific requirements and opportunities, we expect to stimulate targeted practice explorations and focused academic research.

On the practice front, our plans for the next year call for an investigation along the lines of what we did in our B2B Agenda project. We will draw on the insights and experiences of our B2B Board members, lead practitioners, and others focusing on the innovation–marketing connection, and we will use combinations of exploratory interviews, focused workshops (to review emerging findings with these practitioners and selected academic researchers), and a broader practice survey to enrich our findings. We are planning to provide the ISBM community with periodic summaries of the key insights, along with a full report of our findings at the end of the inquiry.

In parallel, our plans on the research front are to initiate a review of the state-of-knowledge. We will use targeted working sessions and other interactions with selected topic experts, as well as broader engagement of the B2B academic community (and input from a simultaneous practitioner investigation) to delineate research needs and priorities.

Organizational Buying Behavior: Our Next Steps

We view this topic as stronger in terms of its research emphasis and thus associate it with a longer timeline. The first step is to delineate the topic and determine a viable approach to address it. To that end, we plan to orchestrate an exploratory academic workshop to be followed by a broader, mini-conference with researchers (possibly involving some selected practitioners at this stage).

These interactions will guide our subsequent actions. Some of our B2B Board academics envisioned that to develop an up-to-date typology of B2B buyers and buying, we need to capture—perhaps through exploratory research and/or a survey—the richness and heterogeneity of buying situations, along with the various nuances and influences that affect them. Such an effort could be followed by a more in-depth assessment of what it takes to be successful in each of the resulting buying situations.

Advancing the Practice of B2B

The ambition of the B2B Leadership Board is to provide direction and foster advances in the knowledge and practice of B2B marketing and, in so doing, elevate its business impact. This project represents our initial effort, and the preceding plans outline our next steps. We welcome feedback and suggestions that could help us move these efforts along, building solid traction for the path ahead.

Fred Wiersema
ISBM Distinguished Fellow and
Chair, B2B Leadership Board
+1 617 932 1165
FredW@B2Bboard.org

Institute for the Study of Business Markets
Penn State
484 Business Building
University Park, PA 16802
+1 814 863 2782
ISBM.org

Printed in Germany
by Amazon Distribution
GmbH, Leipzig